"My friend Daniel Floyd has a passion to reach people for Christ that sets him apart in our generation—as a Pastor and as a leader. Living The Dream, if you let it, will set you free to fall in love with God's purpose for your life."

Steven Furtick
Lead Pastor, Elevation Church & Author of the New York Times bestseller Greater

"Daniel Floyd is one of the most gifted church planters and innovators I've met in the past few years. God is truly doing an amazing work in and through this young man, and this book is a perfect example of God's favor on Daniel. Living The Dream is what all of us want for our lives. However, we sometimes miss that God is our greatest cheerleader and source for success. Daniel shares great truths from the beautiful story of Joseph's life to remind us of God's perfect plan for each of us. Read it, embrace it, live it...it's what God desires for you!"

Jonathan Falwell
Pastor, Thomas Road Baptist Church

"No pretense here, just straight-from-the-gut honesty from a leader whose private world matches his public life. Daniel skillfully unfolds how to live out the dream. It's life-changing wisdom from a man who gets to live his dream every day."

Brad Leeper
President and Principal, Generis

"So many people go through life on mental cruise-control, never thinking about the plan, purpose and dreams God has for them. Daniel Floyd's Living the Dream will help you confront your doubts, fears, and excuses, and challenge you to take practical faith steps that could alter the trajectory of your life. If you've lost your motivation, confidence, or your dream, this book is for you. Daniel helps us re-imagine the work God wants to do in and through us, and he challenges us to live differently in light of God's purpose for our lives."

Mac Lake
Chief Launch Officer, Launch Network

"Daniel Floyd and his team at Lifepoint Church know some- thing about living the dream...they're doing it! And now you can, too! When you open the pages of this book, be prepared to say goodbye to a life of mediocrity and hello to a brand-new way of living. Prepare to start living the dream! The biblical principles Daniel has applied to build a great church are now available to you and me. I know your life is going to be changed by his message."

Stuart Hodges
Lead Pastor of Waters Edge Church

"Daniel Floyd is a gifted communicator and visionary leader who is living his dream. However, he knows life can sometimes keep us awake at night asking, "Why?" In this book, Daniel challenges us to be more than just positive thinkers, and to see that God is at work even when we experience the unexpected!"

Brian Autry
Executive Director, SBC of Virginia

LIVING
THE DREAM

UNCOVER THE PLAN.
FULFILL YOUR PURPOSE.

DANIEL FLOYD

To Dad and Mom:

It's on the shoulders of your faith and prayers that I am now standing. Thank you for teaching me to live with bold faith and to pursue God's dream.

I love you.

CONTENTS

Section 3: Living The Dream

INTRODUCTION

I'll never forget that night as long as I live. It marked me; it is rehearsed in my memory often. All that I had been taught—all that I believed about God—was being tested in that moment. I grew up in a Pastor's home and my parents had taught me God was a good God who had great plans for me. However, that night it didn't feel like God was good and it definitely didn't feel like there were any great plans in my future. How can anything look bright and promising when you're kneeling over your Dad's body, performing chest compressions while praying God doesn't take him? I wanted him to be there for my graduation . . . my wedding . . . the birth of my children. *This is good?* I wondered. *Are these the great plans God has for me? For us?*

Let me back up to a Sunday morning a few years earlier, during my seventh-grade year. My Dad had just finished preaching, and as was customary in smaller churches, he would stand at the back door and greet those who had attended on their way out. However, on this morning, as Dad made his way down the aisle, I saw him reach for help as he almost fell to the floor.

That day began a chain of events which would render my father unable to pastor a church, unable to work, and eventually unable to even leave the house without assistance. Many doctors, tests, procedures, and hospital stays left us without answers. My Dad was sick, and nobody knew how to help him. He suffered for years without much relief and with very little hope.

Fast forward to that terrifying night while I was home visiting from college, when the things I had been taught to believe clashed with the reality of my actual experience. How does a man who had faithfully served God, given generously of himself to those in need, and only wished to see people encounter Jesus end up in this situation? Were these the great plans God had in store for him?

What I didn't realize in that moment was that the answers to my questions would forever shape me and even set the trajectory of my life. The same is true for you. The reality is, we have all experienced moments in which our beliefs clash with our experience. These are the moments when we ask, "Does God really have great things in store for me?" And it is how we answer this question that determines everything. You can allow the circumstances of your existence to choke the life out of your dreams, or you can allow the circumstances of life to shape your dreams. You can answer "no" and settle for less than your full potential or you can answer "yes" and experience the unexpected. It was in my own moment of truth—when the crisis I was experiencing forced me to face this question head on—that I answered, "YES!!"

SECTION ONE
THE BIRTH
OF A DREAM

CHAPTER ONE

CREATED WITH PURPOSE

You are not an accident, and nothing you have experienced has been by chance. A loving God created you with great purpose, for great things. There is a seed of greatness planted inside of you, and you are meant to see that seed grow into a full-grown purpose. There is a dream in there somewhere!

Did you ever have that nightmare where the monster was underneath your bed, and if your feet hit the floor he would get you, but as long as you stayed under the covers you were safe? Not that I was ever afraid as a kid, (I'm trying to make you think I'm braver than I am), but if I *did* have that dream, somehow my covers would become a protective shield against creepy under-the-bed monsters.

Or maybe you dreamed about becoming the next Major League Baseball player. I took my son to see his first Major League game recently, and his first question was, "Could I do that?" Of course my answer was, "You can do whatever you put your mind to do!" We dream of greatness. It's been planted inside us all. Little girls dream of being princesses —or, in the case of my three-year-old daughter, of meeting "Justin Beaver" (also known as Justin Bieber). Okay, maybe that's not such a great dream.

One thing that unites all of us is that we have all dreamed, and our dreams are never ordinary. Yet sadly, somewhere along the line we put away our dreams like toys in the attic. We grew out of them. We traded in those things that breathed life into us—those thoughts or imaginings that ignited fire in our souls—for the ordinary. We settled for what we perceived to be a safe and achievable reality. We stopped risking!

But is that really how it's supposed to be? Or could it be that God has designed you and me, the dreamers, to —in fact—dream? Could it be that lying dormant in your heart is not merely make believe, but a God-given dream, a God-breathed vision? Could it be that God has placed something in your heart so great and so uniquely designed for you that you sense it could be what you were placed on this planet to do? Could it be that God has positioned you in this time and place to achieve something of significance? Could it be that God Himself has ignited the imagination of your soul?

However, for these dreams the monsters are no longer under our beds but now in our hearts and minds, taking the shape of insecurity, doubt, discouragement, and a desire to be in control. Fearing these monsters, we try to stay safe under the covers, never putting our feet on the ground of risk.

There is more to our existence than living safely! God wants to birth something so great, so unexplainable and powerful through your life that it will require you to relinquish your learned perception of assumptions about reality. There is more to life than your 9 to 5 . . . God has a design that includes greatness and influence and impact, and which transcends this world and enters eternity. It's time to pull that dream off the shelf of your mind and allow it to take shape within your heart. It's time to stop making excuses for your lack of pursuit and start living the dream.

Stop worrying about what you don't have! Where you are lacking, God will make up the difference. Lose your concern about where you fall short, for God will lift you up. Stop allowing the mistakes of your past to shape your destiny because you think God will hold them against your future. Simply do ALL of what you CAN do and God will do ALL of what you CAN'T do. Greatness is not defined by power, prestige, or prominence, but rather by reaching your full potential in God and living out your God-given destiny.

Maybe you're a stay-at-home Mom who dreams of raising kids who will be world-changers, but you think that sounds too radical or you don't know how to do it. Maybe you're a student with a dream to impact your school with the love of Jesus and see the lives of your friends drastically changed, but you're unsure of yourself and don't feel equipped. Maybe you're a businessman who dreams of leading the way in caring for the poor — or maybe you dream about starting a new venture but you're uncomfortable not knowing the details of God's plan. Maybe you are a person who possesses an incredible talent that remains dormant in your life because you have come to believe you cannot make a secure living using it. Listen, your job isn't to figure out all the details, to determine how great or small your dream is, or to even feel comfortable taking risks. Your responsibility is simply to begin to pursue the dream God has given you.

The difference between a man or a woman who changes the world forever and one who does nothing is not the possession of a dream, but the courageous execution of it. God has always used common men to accomplish uncommon things, but He requires that they believe He can do this.

Throughout Scripture we see dreamers, but perhaps the most famous one is a young man named Joseph. Chapter 37 in the Old Testament book of Genesis introduces us to seventeen-year-old Joseph, the son of Jacob and Jacob's favorite wife Rachel—the eleventh of twelve sons. As the son of his father's preferred wife, Joseph grew up in a house full of great tension, anger, and jealousy. Genesis 37:3 tells us Jacob loved Joseph more than any of his other sons, and had a richly ornamented coat made for him. When Joseph's brothers saw this, they hated him and couldn't speak a kind word about him.

Yet it was in the midst of everyday turmoil and damaged

familial relationships that Joseph found himself in the right place—he was living under his parents' authority. He was being faithful to what was in front of him—living his life despite severe opposition. And it was within this ordinary setting of hardship and obedience that Joseph had a dream

. . .

> Joseph said, *"Let me tell you about my dream. We were out in the field, tying up bundles of wheat. Suddenly my bundle stood up, and your bundles gathered around and bowed down to it." His brothers asked, "Do you really think you are going to be king and rule over us?" Now they hated Joseph more than ever because of what he had said about his dream.*
>
> *Joseph later had another dream, and he told his brothers, "Listen to what else I dreamed. The sun, the moon, and eleven stars bowed down to me." When he told his father about this dream, his father became angry and said, "What's that supposed to mean? Are your mother and I and your brothers all going to come and bow down in front of you?" Joseph's brothers were jealous of him, but his father kept wondering about the dream.*
>
> Genesis 37:6-11

Joseph had neither the platform nor the notoriety one

might think he would need to receive such a vision from God. Instead, Joseph's dream was birthed in obscurity.

Often it is in a place of insignificance—when no one is looking—that God births and shapes our dreams, so that when everyone is looking we are prepared for our dreams to come to fruition. So it was in this trivial, awkward place that Joseph shared his dream with his brothers.

Maybe you're feeling the way Joseph may have felt and thinking, *Okay, I do have a dream—but now isn't the right time. The situation I'm in and the circumstances I currently face don't create a conducive environment in which to pursue this dream.* Joseph definitely didn't find himself in a situation that embraced his dream, but he realized it was from God.

Perhaps the right time to begin speaking your dream is the moment in which God reveals it to you.

Is it possible that we intentionally refrain from sharing the dream God has placed on our hearts because once it's verbalized, it can't be hidden, and once it is no longer hidden, we are now accountable to pursue it? Or do we fear the opinions of those around us?

Joseph's dream, this new burning passion, this little glimpse of his destiny in God—a thing that excited him, that caused purpose to rise up within him—was the very thing that would create great division in the relationships around him in ways he could not yet foresee or imagine. And this may be true in your life as well. Not everyone will be excited about your dream . . . Some people may get jealous; others may reject your dream or discourage you. It could even be that the people who are closest to you become the people who unintentionally seek to extinguish your passion. Joseph's own family couldn't receive the dream God had placed in his heart.

These interactions with Joseph's family were only the early warning signs of the great price this dream would cost him. The greater the dream, the greater the price you pay to realize it. This price is not necessarily in terms of monetary cost, but in terms of the work God must do in you—not only to be the one who births the dream, but also the person who sees the dream fulfilled.

But what will happen if you don't dare to dream? What life will not be touched? What child will not be loved? What business will never get off the ground? What art will never be formed? What void will be created—in your life, your family, your community, your church—if you allow opposition to keep you from dreaming?

CHAPTER TWO

UNLIKELY CANDIDATE

Maybe you agree and can think of several people this applies to—but you're not ready to believe *you're* one of them. Maybe it's a lack of confidence in your ability. Maybe it's your stage in life. Maybe choices in your past diminish your belief that God could or would do great things through you.

Joseph was an unlikely candidate, too—the next to last among twelve brothers and the most hated of the family. He didn't seem like the premier choice God would use to save a nation!

Or how about Peter, one of the people who spent the most time with Jesus while He was on this earth? Peter had the honor of seeing with his own eyes the dead raised back to life, blinded eyes opened, and a lame man walking. However, it was Peter who denied Jesus three times and was at a loss after the death of Jesus. Another of Jesus' disciples, John, writes of a situation in which Peter returned to fishing after Jesus' crucifixion, even though Jesus had called him to be a "fisher of men."

Talk about a vision for your life!

Talk about clarity for your dream!

Jesus Himself walked up to Peter and said, "Here is the direction for your life. I am going to make you a fisher of men." But now, even after seeing the miraculous, Peter has returned to his former life.

I imagine Peter was thinking, *Even if He did rise from the dead, I don't know if I'm even qualified to be His friend anymore, let alone in His inner circle. Even if He does come back and the Kingdom of God happens and everything plays out the way that He said it would, I've rejected Him at the moment He needed me the most. I am not a qualified candidate to be on His team again.*

How many of us have stopped dreaming great dreams for God because we think we're not qualified? It's not that we don't dream, it's that our dreams are stolen by our own negative thinking. John continues with the story, saying that as Peter was out fishing, Jesus showed up on the shore for another conversation about fishing. He asked, "Did you catch any fish?" And they answered, "No." Jesus replied, "Why don't you try throwing your nets on the other side?" I wonder if Peter thought, I've heard this before. And then John said to him, "Peter, it's the Lord." And in that moment, Peter grabbed his coat, jumped out of the boat, and started running to Jesus.

He jumped out of his comfort zone.

He jumped out of what he had known.

Three years earlier, Peter had gone from comfort to calling, only to return to comfort again. But this encounter with Jesus compelled him back to a place of calling.

And he jumped at the chance.

That's exactly what your response should be. Jesus is standing on the shore of your life, calling you to greatness and encouraging you to reclaim your dream. Your response must be to leave what is comfortable and run after the dream God has for you. You were not placed on this earth to play it safe. A faith that plays it safe is not a real faith. God invites us to take risks, to walk by faith, to get out of our comfort zone and believe for great things.

Peter approaches the shore and has this conversation with Jesus: "Peter, do you love me?" And Peter answers, "Lord, you know I love you." It's a significant moment for Peter. Jesus says, "Then feed my sheep." And He asks him again, "Peter, do you love me?" And Peter says, "You know I love you." Jesus is communicating, "If you love me, don't go back to the familiar. I have so much more for you than that. Go to what I've called you to—go feed my sheep."

Peter did that very thing and God used him to preach a powerful sermon on the day of Pentecost in which 3,000 people came to faith in Christ. What if Peter had decided to go back to the fishing business?

What will not happen in your life if you decide to go back

to what's comfortable? I'm praying that God draws a line in the sand for you and you step over it and you're never the same, because God did not design you to simply exist. Receive today a dose of holy determination to run after God's dream for you.

It's in you.

God has chosen you.

And the world is waiting for you!

SECTION TWO

THE PROCESS IS
THE POINT

CHAPTER THREE
LEFT OVER PIECES

Now that I'm a parent, I have the privilege of exploring the great world of toy assembly—including my favorites that come with fast food (insert sarcasm here). I am also becoming an expert in the assembly of furniture. My wife and I love a good trip to IKEA, where furniture in a box becomes a spiritual exercise in patience. It never fails that after completing an IKEA project, I find myself with a handful of extra wooden pieces and screws. It is at this point that, because I don't want the furniture to collapse or the toy to fall apart and injure my child, I retrieve the instructions out of the trash and start over.

These moments always remind me that the process is as important as the product. The process of putting this thing together is extremely important. As a matter of fact, without the process, the product is faulty at best—and destructive at worst.

In the pursuit of your dream, the same principle applies: God is just as concerned about *who you are* as you pursue His dream for you as He is about *what you do*. And because of that, He will take you through a process of shaping.

I believe that God is not only the One who gives the dream, but also the One who shapes the heart of the dreamer, and that shaping is crucially important if we are ever to fulfill His calling. Reaching our full potential in God is dependent on the time we have spent being shaped by Him.

Too many of us stop short of becoming all God wants us to be when we resist this process. We live in a stage and an age in which we want it microwaved. We want it yesterday. We don't even want to get out of our cars to order our food! And for the most part, we actually can get what we want, when we want it. The landscape of our culture feeds into this mentality and creates the expectation in each of us that this is how life works.

However, in God's economy, character isn't shaped in 30 seconds or less. You don't get the spotlight immediately and the dream is rarely fulfilled overnight. Because God has your best interest at heart, He will take you through a process by which He shapes your heart and your character.

Because that, in turn, will shape your dream.

NO MICROWAVED DREAMS

Moses is a great example of God taking a man through a

heart-shaping process in order to use him greatly. You may have heard the story or seen the Prince of Egypt movie. Moses stands before Pharaoh—the most powerful man in the world at that time—and boldly says, "Pharaoh, Pharaoh—Oh Baby, let my people go!"

Well, maybe he didn't say it in those exact words, but you get the point. This was Moses' moment in the spotlight. This was his moment to do something great for God. He was the one appointed and anointed to lead the people of Israel out of slavery and bondage.

What courage it must have taken for Moses to stand before the Pharaoh and demand the freedom of his people. To really grasp the audacity of this demand, you must understand that the children of Israel were the entire workforce in Pharaoh's kingdom. They provided the labor needed to keep his economy going. Moses knew that Pharaoh would surely wonder if Moses had lost his mind. And who was he to speak on behalf of God, anyway? Moses must have had to battle those thoughts and dig deep to be so bold.

But Moses' story didn't start there.

This moment for Moses was shaped by previous experiences that may have been even more important.

Moses' life story is detailed in the book of Exodus, beginning in the first chapter. He was born into an Israelite family during a time in which the reigning Pharaoh had sent out an edict to kill all the Israelite baby boys. Through a series of God-ordained events, Moses was adopted by the daughter of the current Pharaoh and raised in the royal family. Moses grew up in the palace with many of the accoutrements of life to which very few of us are accustomed. For 40 years, Moses lived in the palace, until the day he witnessed a fellow Hebrew—a slave of the Pharaoh's—being beaten and abused. Enraged with anger, Moses flew to the man's defense and killed the perpetrator, who was one of Pharaoh's men. As a result of this criminal act, Moses fled from the palace . . .

From his place of power . . .

From being a prince in Egypt . . .

To the desert.

This desert would become a 40-year classroom for Moses, which would prepare him to later fulfill his destiny.

It's on the edge of this desert that Moses meets Zipporah, the daughter of a priest named Jethro. He begins to work for Jethro as a shepherd and eventually marries Zipporah, becoming Jethro's son-in-law. Moses' journey takes him from the palace to poverty—from having status in the community to tending to the needs of sheep. It's a "riches to rags" story.

Many of us would see a journey like that as anything but forward movement, but in God's economy, the process is progress. If the process takes you from the palace to tending sheep, it's still progress in God's eyes. He is concerned about your process because it is the tool with which He will shape your character.

The process will not be easy. You will be faced with circumstances along the way in which you will have to trust God, learn difficult lessons, and be patient. You will have opportunities to respond with faith and obedience, allowing God to strengthen you through your circumstances, or to become bitter and faithless, trying to take matters into your own hands.

The process and how you respond to it are key players in the production of your God-given dream; because God will not produce anything that is faulty at best and destructive at worst.

ARE YOU AVAILABLE?

While faithfully tending Jethro's sheep, Moses led the flock to the far side of the wilderness and came to Horeb, the mountain of God. There, he saw a bush that was on fire—but he noticed that in spite of the fire, the bush didn't actually burn. Intrigued, Moses approached the bush, at which point something even more unusual happened: When God saw that Moses had gone over to look at the bush, He called to him from within it, "Moses! Moses!" And Moses answered, "Here I am."

Can you imagine how Moses must have been feeling about his life at this point? He had gone from living in a palace with servants who met his every need to walking sheep through a desert and meeting their every need. However, Moses remained faithful to do what God had put in front of him to do.

I think many of us miss our destinies because when we walk through the desert seasons of our lives, we forget to be faithful to what is in front of us. We tend not to want to do the hard work of preparation that often comes in those seasons, but I believe God is looking for our level of availability over our level of capability. The question to ask yourself is, are you available—no matter the task?

We like things that are easy. However, if it were easy to build a multimillion-dollar business, wouldn't everybody be building one? If it were easy to have a family who loves God and to raise kids with a heritage of knowing, loving, and serving Jesus, then everybody would be doing it. It's not easy to do that. It takes hard work in the desert seasons. And it's the love of God that allows us to experience those seasons.

It is the love of God that shapes you, so that when you get to the moment where the spotlight is on you, you don't fall on your face. When you get to that moment, you can handle it—you can be bold and even audacious about it, because your character has been shaped in the desert.

Many of us don't want to go through the desert, so we stop short of fulfilling all that God wants to do in us. The desert is difficult. It's dry; the ground is hard.

But it is there that your heart is shaped and your destiny is determined.

CHAPTER FOUR
YES, BUT!

Have you ever heard someone say, "If I had his or her talent, resources, and opportunity, then I would be able to do what he or she is doing"? We seem to wait for some elusive moment when we will have the right combination of resources, talent, and opportunity. We say, "God, we are willing to do whatever you want... but... !"

We have a *yes, but* approach to obedience.

The reality is that if you wait for the time when everything aligns and you have all you need to accomplish the job, you will be waiting your entire life. You are never going to have all the talent you need, all the resources you need or all the opportunities you need. If you did, you wouldn't have to rely on God—and as you pursue your dream, God will never create a situation that keeps you from needing Him.

Moses was available, but to a certain point. He had come to grips with his current employment but now God was calling him to something greater.

God was calling him to become the deliverer of His people.

We would like to think that had we been in Moses' shoes, we would have fallen on our faces before God in full surrender to His purpose and His plan for us. We think, *If God gave me a burning bush moment, I would know His will and I would follow it without hesitation.* However, we seem unable to do some of the simplest things in the Christian life . . . forgiving others, being gracious, and showing honor. Could it be that by simply obeying what is already revealed, we would receive revelation about the things in our lives that seem hidden?

Moses was presented with an amazing opportunity, yet his first response was, "But God—who am I?" A lack of confidence stood between Moses and his God assignment. How often has a lack of confidence in your abilities or resources stopped you before you ever started? Do you wonder sometimes if you really heard from God at all?   I believe that if God created you with a purpose, He will empower you at the right time to fulfill that purpose.

And I believe that should bolster confidence in your heart.

I'm not talking about a *pick-yourself-up-by-your-bootstraps* kind of confidence. It's not an, "I can do better, I am better, and gosh darn it, people like me" type of confidence. It is confidence in who you are in God, and confidence in the One who created and called you.

Whenever I would leave the house for school or a friend's house as a child, my mom and dad would say, "Remember whose you are—you're a King's Kid." I knew exactly what they meant. They were reminding me that I belonged to Jesus and that I should think, act and live like it—that I should live with confidence.

Having confidence doesn't mean I won't face situations and circumstances that scare the life out of me. In fact, if the dream you sense God calling you to pursue doesn't make you feel as though you're going vomit a little (excuse the crudeness but you get the point, right?), it might not quite be big enough.

On February 8th, 2012, I was talking with a friend and mentor of mine, sharing some things about the growth of our church and how our newly-added third service had filled up in a matter of two weeks. Our church was once again at a crossroads, and we needed to do something to create more space. We were already planning to open another location in the fall, but I was looking for my friend's advice on what to do in the meantime.

My friend listened patiently and then asked, "Are you ready to hear my thoughts?" And I thought, *I'm not sure*, but I said, "Absolutely." He said, "I would open that second campus on Easter Sunday, April 8th."

He was suggesting we open our second location, completely duplicating everything we did as a church, in the next sixty days. In that moment I sensed my friend's counsel was from the Lord, but my second thought was, *I think I'm going to vomit.* I had a decision to make. I could think of all the reasons it wouldn't work; I could operate by fear and make excuses; or I could have confidence in God's leading and make a move in God's direction.

Living with confidence does not mean you won't experience fear, doubt, or second guesses. If you are human, you will have those emotions. However, it is your willingness to move forward with a mentality that says, "whatever the request, the answer is yes." God really is looking for your availability over your capability. And it is when we say "Yes" that the miracles of God are unleashed.

God moved in amazing ways and allowed us to open our second portable campus in 60 days, just as my friend suggested. Our "yes" response to God was in both faith and action; we created the infrastructure, recruited the leaders, trained the volunteers, bought the equipment, learned the technology, rented another school, and installed fiber optics between the two locations in order to broadcast live. On Easter Sunday, we launched with more than 1300 people in the new location, over 70 of whom placed their faith in Jesus that weekend. It was miraculous, and God allowed us to witness it all because we traded our "Yes, but . . ." for, "Whatever the request, the answer is yes."

CHAPTER FIVE
IT'S IN FRONT OF YOU

Have you ever tried to help someone, only to wonder later if they really wanted your help in the first place? I was recently asked, "Pastor, I'm looking for a job. We're in a tough situation and really need the money. Do you know anybody who's hiring? I'll do just about anything." I responded that I would certainly let this person know if I heard of anything that might help.

A few weeks later, I happened to hear someone say they were looking for help in a somewhat remedial task. Although it wasn't a high-paying job, it would, at minimum, pay some bills. I referred the individual to the job and told him he should check it out, and I even recommended him to the potential employer. I said, "It may not be your dream job, but it will put money in the bank until you are able get into the field you were hoping for."

A few weeks later I checked in on this man and asked,

"Hey, did you ever end up taking that job?"

His reply: "No, it just wasn't what I wanted to do."

As I have gotten a little older, I have learned to filter my thoughts prior to allowing them to leave my mouth. However, I was thinking, *You need a job! You need to put food on the table. You're in a desert season right now—I know it's tough, but. . . it's not what you wanted to do? Are you kidding me?? How can you expect God to open greater doors of opportunity when you're not willing to walk through the smaller doors He opens?*

I believe this is why Moses got the job of leading God's people out of slavery. In the desert season of his life, Moses was giving his all to what was in front of him. He wasn't sitting back in the desert season of his life saying, "Well, whenever God shows up in a burning bush with an amazing assignment for me, then I'll do something." Moses was in the desert season with no light at the end of the tunnel, no change in sight, and certainly no sign of an opportunity to lead an entire enslaved people group to freedom. Moses didn't know it, but all of that was on the horizon for him.

And meanwhile, he was faithfully watching Jethro's sheep.

Idleness does not grab the attention of God. Moses was active. He put his hand to what was in front of him, which in turn put him right in the place where he would encounter God in a burning bush.

Had he not been watching Jethro's sheep, he would never

have led them to the desert of Horeb.

Had he not been in the desert of Horeb, he would not have seen the burning bush.

Had he not seen the burning bush, he would have missed the calling from God.

Had Moses missed the calling from God, he would also have missed the opportunity to lead the nation of Israel to freedom.

Had Moses been sitting on the couch, flipping the channels on his remote control and waiting for God to make a burning bush appear in his living room, he would never have lived the dream God had for him.

In the desert season, when what we thought would be our reality does not come to fruition, it is crucially important for us to be active. It's imperative that we put our hand to what God has put in front of us, whatever it is. Whether you like it or not, whether it's glamorous or not, whether it requires the skills you already have or not, embrace what God has in front of you right now, because if you are not faithful in the desert you will miss the opportunity to be fruitful on the other side of it.

I'm fully convinced that it's not a superior skill set that will change the world—it's people who have hearts that are available to do whatever God wants them to do, whenever and wherever God wants them to do it.

Moses was not only active, but he was also available to God. Think about Moses' perspective at that time—there was no end in sight. If the purpose of God for his life was to simply serve Jethro by watching over the sheep so Jethro could serve as the Priest of Midian, that's what Moses was going to do.

There was no word from the Lord for Moses that one day there would be a burning bush. There was no plan that told Moses, "If you'll just watch these sheep for forty years, I will intersect your life in an encounter that will not only give you purpose and destiny but will radically change the course of history." Moses couldn't have known that was in the plan. But he was available, far more available than many of us are—most of us can't last even forty *days* in our desert seasons!

Don't you think Moses had a greater skill set than what was required for being a shepherd? He had grown up in the palace. He probably had been given a great education. He very likely would have had a sophisticated understanding of society and culture. He hadn't spent his nights sleeping at the gate of a sheepfold and his skill level, educational level, and understanding of social situations were probably much higher than that of an ordinary shepherd. Moses might have looked at the situation and said, "God . . . You know, I think I'm more qualified to do something during these forty years than tend a bunch of sheep for my father-in-law." And Moses would have been correct in that assessment.

But God is not concerned about how well you can do something; He is concerned about how willing you are—how surrendered your heart and your life are to Him.

Your abilities don't impress God.

Your humility does.

And your availability is tested when God places you in a position for which you are over-qualified. Are you willing to do something that, in your perception, is below your skill level?

I have seen this availability principle over and over again during the seven years since we planted our church. Growing churches attract lots of people, and every once in a while, we attract people who have their own agendas. Maybe their former church wouldn't allow them to do something, so they show up ready to tell us God's vision for a certain area of this ministry. Many times, that vision doesn't line up with the vision God has given our church, so we share that truth while offering other opportunities for them within the context of what God has called us to do here. Nine times out of ten, the response is, "Well, that's just not what I'm gifted to do," or, "We really feel like God is leading us to another church. . ." The skill level isn't the issue. What is being tested is the heart.

God is looking for a heart that says, "Whatever door You open for me, that's the one I'm going to walk through, whether it's great, grand, small or insignificant." If we think we are too big or important or gifted or well trained to do what is remedial, we are really too small to do what is great!

I learned this principle in my very first ministry job. The

church I worked for held its growing student ministry services at a firehouse, and every Wednesday night I showed up to set up the chairs. It never crossed my mind to look at the student pastor and say, "I'm just not gifted to set up chairs." It was what was available for me to do, and I wanted to be engaged in what God was doing, so I set up chairs. And I set them up with excellence, making sure the rows were lined up and an equal number of chairs were in each row. It wasn't glamorous. I never once was on the platform. I never even led a small group. I simply set up the chairs!

I didn't know it in the moment, but I'm thoroughly convinced that because I was available then to set up the chairs, God has entrusted me now to lead what Outreach Magazine listed in 2012 as #22 of the top 100 fastest growing churches in America. I simply did what was in front of me during that season. Sometimes I look back over the past seven years—at the thousands of people I have had the privilege of seeing come to faith in Christ—and I don't think about the growth we've experienced.

I don't think about my preaching.

I don't think about my leadership skills.

All I can think about is setting up those chairs.

It's not about your skill level or how much knowledge you have . . . God is not impressed! It's about your heart and your character. It's about God shaping you to be able to withstand the responsibility that comes with the blessing of living the dream. The key is being completely abandoned to saying, "God, whatever it is You want to do with me, whenever and however You want to do it with me—whether it's in the spotlight or in some back hallway, I just want to be available to you."

When you think of dreaming great dreams for God, what is it that motivates you? The desert season will strip back and reveal your motives. Motive is that underlying thing that drives us to do what we do—it's what wakes us up, causes us to push, and inspires us to give our time, energy and resources to the dream. And the scary thing about our motives is that we can candy-coat them with spiritual rhetoric and fool everyone—including ourselves.

Are you motivated to build a platform so that your name will be known, or to fulfill some unmet personal need? Are you motivated by a reaction inside you or by proving a point against something or someone?

Or are you motivated by glorifying God in everything you do?

Are you willing to set up chairs?

BEFORE YOU GET THE KEYS

For Moses, tending sheep wouldn't be the end of the story. In the burning bush, God said, "Moses, Moses." When God calls your name twice, it's important. Moses answered, "Here I am." He wasn't making a geographical declaration —he was revealing his heart. *Here I am. I smell like sheep.*

I murdered a guy 40 years ago and ran from it. I've lived in the palace and I've lived in the desert, and here I am. I'm convinced Moses was ready for that burning bush moment because he hadn't resisted the process.

And what about you? What is it that you know God wants you to do about which you're pushing back against? What shaping do you sense God trying to do in you that you're resisting? What is the conversation you know you need to have that you're putting off?

Is there someone you need to forgive?

Is there stuff that needs to be stripped away?

Don't resist it, because resisting the process could mean forfeiting your dream. Your destiny will be faulty at best and useless at worst if you resist the process.

At the age of four, my son became interested in the car. He is interested in everything about it—how it runs, what makes it work, the purpose of each of the buttons and levers and gauges. Now, at the age of five, he wants to help me pump gas. And of course, it doesn't stop there—he wants to drive sometimes. So I let him; on a long country driveway with no other cars around, I'll put him in my lap and let him turn the wheel while I manage the gas and the brakes. And he loves it. He thinks it's the greatest thing and feels like the biggest boy in the world.

I love to see him light up when he takes the wheel and thinks he has control of the car (of course my wife is sitting in the passenger seat with her eyes closed). Because I love him, I find great joy in seeing my son experience great joy. If you are a parent, you know that feeling—there are no words to describe how we love our children.

However, the love I have for my son means that I only allow him to "drive" on my lap, on a long country driveway with no other cars around. I would never allow him at this age to have the keys to a car or drive one by himself. It's his dream. He really wants to drive. But it's not going to happen, because I love him. He needs to mature in the areas of reflexes and decision-making and hand-eye coordination before it would be safe for him to drive. He doesn't have the capacity to understand the power of driving thousands of pounds of metal down the interstate. I do, and because I know more than he does about driving a car—and because I love him beyond words—I am not going to give him the keys to his dream. . . yet.

But I am going to let him crank it up every once in a while. I am going to let him sit in my lap and hold the wheel every so often, because I want to shape him. I want to mold him. I want him to be ready, so that on the day he does pull out of the garage on his own, I will have confidence that he's ready to go. I want to know I haven't put him in danger by letting him fulfill his dream.

I believe that is how God is with us. He's not going to give us the keys to our dream until we're willing to go through the process. He knows we need to grow and mature and be shaped. There's no way He would hand us the keys to our

dream before we are ready, because He knows how danger-
ous it could be for us if we are unprepared.

So it is out of His great love for us that God takes us
through a process—a season of preparation. The desert isn't
His judgment on you. The desert is His blessing to you because He loves you so dearly. He wants to prepare you, so
that when the day comes for you to stand up and say, "Pharaoh, let my people go," you've got the confidence of God in
you. You will be bold on that day because you will have been
shaped by God in your desert season, and you will know that
He's with you and working in and through you.

When the moment arrives, it will be too late to prepare.
Now is the time.

Because the process really is just as important as the
product.

CHAPTER SIX

NOT WHAT I EXPECTED

The journey to your dream is often peppered with moments that take you by surprise, catch you off guard, and knock the breath right out of you. These are the moments when the reality of life collides with your expectations. We all walk through life with hope that things will play out a certain way. We have many expectations . . .

Expectations of what our financial future will look like.

Expectations for the relationships we will have and how they will make us feel.

Expectations for our work environment, where we will live, and what we will do.

Expectations of God.

When these expectations are met, life is good, God is good, and our perspective is positive. On the other hand, when these expectations are not met, we feel life is difficult,

God is distant and uncaring, and our outlook for the future is dim. It's important to get a grip on this, though, because reality is rarely what we were expecting.

Maybe this is evident in your marriage. You met, you fell in love, you sprang for the ring, and had a Hollywood wedding.

You dreamed of the life you would have, the house you would buy, what she would wear to bed (something made of satin or silk) and wouldn't wear (anything made of cotton or flannel).

You named the kids together and even named the dog. You just knew that you would share conversation and coffee every morning before work and make love every night. She just knew that every day you would come home from work and joyfully take the kids so she could enjoy a Calgon bath.

But now here you are, one month, two years, ten years down the road—and it's not what you expected.

Maybe you are single and thought by now you would be married. The single life is not as easy and free as everyone makes it out to be. All you want is a lasting relationship with someone who is committed to you, but your current reality is not what you expected. Maybe you or a loved one are battling a physical illness and the reality of your struggle is with you from the moment you wake up to the moment you go to bed and often throughout the night. An answer to your constant prayer for relief is nowhere to be found, and life is just not what you expected.

In our story of Joseph, we find that he faced this same dichotomy. He had received a great dream from God, but found himself in a holding pattern. If he believed his dream, things were certainly not shaking out as expected. There was no path to power in sight. But even without clarity for the future, Joseph remained faithful to the things that were in front of him. Working faithfully for his father, Joseph had to prove himself trustworthy in the little things. Only then would God promote him to greater things, because God will only entrust you with that which you can be entrusted.

And this requires testing.

None of us would willingly sign up for this type of testing. Many of us would rather run the company ourselves, thinking we could do a better job of managing the organization than our bosses. But the real question is, do you have the capacity to be faithful in the cubicle to which you are currently assigned? Are you giving 100% to that which God has currently entrusted you, even while no one is looking?

You want to have children who love Jesus and live for Him. But do you seek Him personally? Do your kids know that God's house is a priority in your house? Do they learn what a passionate pursuit of God looks like by observing your life?

You want to deeply connect with God and be used greatly to influence others with God's love. Maybe you want to possess a great understanding of God's Word or experience great victory over a certain sin. But are you faithful to open your Bible, read it, memorize it, and allow it to change you? Are you faithful to spend time in prayer, seeking God's heart? Are you faithful to open yourself up to accountability? God doesn't skip steps on the journey to your dream, but you may attempt to circumvent the process.

Maybe you think you are above a certain step. This is called pride, which God calls sin. Maybe you think you have matured beyond a certain stage and can chart your own course toward the destiny God has for you. But the reality is that you won't be elevated to the next level until you have been faithful at your current level.

This isn't about having to work to seek the approval of God. God accepts you and loves you just the way you are. This is about the truth that God will only entrust to you that which He knows you can be entrusted. Your faithfulness in a seemingly insignificant and mundane assignment reveals your capacity to be trusted with greater things.

And those who can be trusted are promoted.

SOMETHING HAS TO CHANGE

Joseph's father sends him out to check on his brothers at Shechem, where they had taken their flocks. Shechem was a place of abundance, known for its vast vegetation, which made the twenty-hour trip worthwhile. Joseph obeys the instruction of his father and makes the trip.

Knowing his brothers hate him.

Knowing he is walking into a hostile environment.

We are often asked to do uncomfortable things as part of God's heart-shaping process. These aren't meaningless exercises, but rather character-building, passion-imparting moments. Passion isn't truly revealed when emotions are high and excitement is flowing, but when you are asked to swim upstream.

Your character is shaped when you follow through with what God asks you to do in spite of your feelings.

It's easy to obey and worship God when everything is going your way, but how easy is it when your father asks you to take a twenty-hour journey to check on your brothers who would rather see you dead?

What if Joseph had not obeyed his father, and decided to stay home instead of doing the hard thing? We have no way of knowing, but I believe there is a good chance he would never have realized his dream. Many times we fall short of realizing our dream because in the process, we resist the hard things God asks us to do, and therefore we get stuck.

God asks you to forgive so that you can lay down that baggage. God asks you to reconcile past hurts so that you can move on. God asks you to get your house in order and begin leading your family. God asks you to be faithful with your finances so you can live under His blessing.

God will often ask us to surrender the part of ourselves we have made off limits to Him. And if we stay stuck because of our resistance to the process, we trade God's best for our comfort. We trade God's will for our own control, and become more stubborn than useful! We murder opportunity, day after day, by resisting sacrifice and allowing the clock to tick on our obedience.

Sacrifice isn't an experience we readily embrace, but intuitively, we know that great opportunities require great sacrifice if we are ever to reap a great reward. One Sunday recently, our church presented a new global partnership we had developed in Guatemala. I challenged our church to help over two thousand Guatemalans by removing the very shoes they were wearing and donating them right then and there. Over 2500 pairs of shoes were left behind as people walked barefoot out of church that morning. It was a powerful sight.

My wife and I wanted to involve our children, five-year-old Owen and three-year-old Faith, in the initiative. Owen was an easy sell. Upon learning there were kids his age without shoes that God wanted us to help, he was all in! Faith was a different story. She immediately let us know that those were her shoes and she was not about to give them up, to which Owen responded, "Faith, you're not being very nice; you need to give your shoes because we are supposed to help God's loved ones." I'm not sure where he got the "God's loved ones" phrase, but his message to his sister was very simple: there are people in need and we should help them, even if it means we have to sacrifice something.

Sacrifice has a great payout in the end. For Owen, the payout was helping "God's loved ones," because great opportunities require great sacrifice but bring a great reward. We will never see the reward if we don't embrace the sacrifice.

We have trouble embracing the sacrifice when we value what we are being called to sacrifice more than we value the reward. The change such a sacrifice would require of us might be a price we are not willing to pay. Our vision is shortsighted because the momentary loss seems to outweigh the future reward.

For Joseph, the sacrifice he made paled in comparison with the reward God had for him. But the reward would have never been realized unless something changed.

Joseph had to change.

You have to change.

You can't get to where God wants you to be if you remain in your current location. The old-timers in East Tennessee where I grew up have a phrase: "You can't get there from here." It means if you are to make it to your destination, something is going to have to change. There is a lot of truth to that statement on the journey to your dream. If you are going to realize the reward, something has to change.

You can't keep doing life the way you have been doing it. You can't continue with the same behavior and the same mindset. Something has to change, and change requires sacrifice. Are you willing to do the hard thing—to relinquish comfort—in order to pursue God's dream?

If the answer is yes, then the possibilities are endless,

and the ride of your life is about to begin!

CHAPTER SEVEN

UNUSUAL PROMOTION

Joseph made his way out to his brothers, where they had moved beyond Shechem to a place called Dothen. As he approached his brothers they could see him coming from a long way off, and they plotted to kill him.

And you thought your family was dysfunctional.

Can you imagine the mumbling as Joseph approaches? "Here comes the dreamer; here comes Dad's favorite. Can you believe he has the gall to come out here?"

Don't be surprised if you experience the same thing. There are people in your life who will want to kill your dream. The change in you will create an uncomfortable climate for those in your life who are unwilling to change. Your progress will reveal their apathy, and that will not go over well. But if you will stay the course, their pushback will actually push you forward.

As Joseph approached his brothers, they actually began plotting to kill him. Reuben, the eldest brother, suggested a different plan—to throw Joseph into a pit and stain his beloved coat with animal blood so their father would think he was dead.

A better plan than murder, but still not very charitable.

Joseph walks right into a trap set by his brothers, and the very thing placing him in this position is his obedience to his father. He arrives to accomplish his father's assignment and his brothers grab him, rip off his coat, and throw him into a pit.

Can you imagine how Joseph feels? Bruised and beaten, lying in the bottom of a pit at the hands of his own brothers, he probably thought, *This doesn't look like my brothers bowing down to me.* He may have prayed, "God, this is nothing like the dream you gave me. How could you tease me by extending promises to me in a dream and then allow this to take place?"

Joseph probably thought it was over, with no hope, no return to the dream he once had. Have you ever been in that place?

Where you feel alone, abandoned, and abused?

Where there is no light at the end of your tunnel?

Where your dream is dead on arrival?

Joseph's uncertainty about his future must have felt like having the wind knocked out of him. Not only does it appear that his dream will never come true, but now he has been left for dead in a pit. Could it be that this was all part of the process?

God was stripping some things away from Joseph.

God was positioning Joseph in a place of total dependency on Him.

Joseph's pit was actually a promotion.

I think back to that season when my Dad was battling what turned out to be a rare disease. It was painful, it was dark, and it was even lonely at times. As a result of his illness, Dad was no longer able to work. Each day brought new challenges and new stressors. People we thought would be there to walk with us through difficulty were nowhere to be found. There were days when we felt like we, too, were thrown into a pit. Maybe you have felt that way as well.

But during that season we learned to trust God on a deeper level. During that season our faith was stretched, and we drew closer to God than ever before.

I heard my Dad say that he wouldn't trade what God did during that time for anything. He told me personally that he would go through the battle of that disease all over again in order to know God and experience Him the way he did later. In hindsight, that season of sickness was a gift.

It was preparation.

God will never create a life for you that will make Him inconsequential. Instead, if you allow Him, God will promote you to greater levels of intimacy with Him and greater opportunities to be used by Him. And you just might discover you experience the promotion in the strangest places.

What Joseph didn't know was that God was beginning

a process of causing some things to die in Joseph so his dream could live. God was stripping away pride in order to give birth to humility. He was allowing fear to die so faith could live. These things in Joseph had to die if God's dream for him was ever to live. So God gave him the first of many unusual promotions.

Let me ask you this: What is it in your life that needs to die so your dream can live? Is it pride? Fear? Insecurity? Jealousy? Until you are willing to allow those things to die, God will not trust you with the greater things your dream promises. But embracing the process of unusual promotion allows God Himself to prepare you to live the dream.

MEANWHILE MOMENT

Joseph's situation is about to go from bad to worse. Rather than kill him, his brothers decided to sell him to a band of merchants passing by, who in turn took him to Egypt to be sold again as a slave. Remember that Joseph is in this predicament because he shared a dream God had given him. He is in a pit because he obeyed the will of his father and was faithful to an assignment. This is not what Joseph thought he deserved. This was certainly not what he expected.

Talk about depending on God! Joseph's brothers took his coat back, covered in blood, and told their father, "He is dead." There would be no search party, no hope that Joseph would be found and rescued. He was utterly rejected and in complete despair. You may be thinking, if this is what it's like to live the dream, count me out! Joseph was probably thinking the same thing. What Joseph didn't know was that God was using the merchants to whom he was sold as taxi drivers to his next destination on the journey. It was not what he expected, but it was exactly what God had planned.

"Meanwhile . . . " the story continues, the merchants sell Joseph to a man named Potiphar—the Captain of the Palace Guard.

Meanwhile.

In other words, at the same moment Joseph's brothers were declaring him dead, God was at work in Joseph's life. Meanwhile, while Joseph couldn't see what was next, when Joseph thought all hope was lost . . . meanwhile . . . God was up to something big!

In this journey of God shaping your heart there will be "meanwhile" moments in which God is orchestrating something big behind the scenes. In those moments, you will experience things you may not understand, but God is working on your behalf. *Meanwhile* may not be what you expect, but it's exactly what God has planned!

CHAPTER EIGHT

MAKING GOD BIG

I spent most of my childhood living in eastern Tennessee. I attended Gravely Elementary School, and it was there, in my fifth grade year, that I participated in my first (and last) talent show. Some of my football teammates and I decided that for our talent, we would perform what was then an epic song—the "Super Bowl Shuffle."

We looked the part, decked out in our football pants, pads and Chicago Bears jerseys, ready to give the lip-syncing performance of our lives.

Until it was our turn to take the stage.

What I remember most about that day is I almost didn't take that step onto the stage—I almost backed out at the last minute. I can still remember my heart pounding with anxiety at the thought of standing before my peers and doing this dance. I just knew we were about to make fools of ourselves and become the butt of every cruel elementary school joke in the county. I almost backed out of the whole thing for fear of what people would think about me.

Have you ever experienced a moment when you almost didn't do something because of your perception of what others might think? Maybe it wasn't in elementary school; maybe it was in middle school or high school. Maybe it was just last week. Either you almost didn't do it, or you actually backed out and missed an opportunity because of what you thought other people would think about you.

One thing I've learned personally (and maybe you're in this boat too) is that as we grow and theoretically mature, some things don't change. As adults, there are still times when we choose our course of action based on the opinions of others. We choose to act—or not act—solely on the basis of what we assume someone might think about us.

This concern about the opinions of others greatly influences our decisions. Maybe you bought a home in your neighborhood because you wanted others to believe something about you. Or perhaps you didn't buy in a different neighborhood because of what someone might have thought about you for living there. Maybe when you looked in your closet this morning, your choice of outfits was influenced by what someone at work would think. Let's face it, the first question we ask when trying on an outfit is, "How does this make me look?" We care a great deal about the opinions of others.

Have you ever been at a church service or event where

you felt led to worship God with abandon, but because of what someone else might think, you held back from your desire to express your love for God?

Or maybe you need to have a difficult conversation with someone, but because of your fear about what he or she may think about you, you refuse to address the issue or you keep putting it off.

Many of us are so paralyzed by our concern with the opinions of others that we avoid making decisions and are inhibited from advancing in certain areas of our lives.

Some people seem to take the opposite extreme. These are the people you hear saying things like, "I don't care what anybody thinks!" In fact, they are so over the top about it that I'm convinced they care even more than the rest of us! And at the end of the day, on some level we all care what people think.

We may not want to care, but we do, because rejection hurts. Criticism hurts. It makes sense that those things would hurt. If you ever get to a place in your life where rejection and criticism don't hurt, something has died inside of you. It's the human experience to feel these things. It's how God made us. Being rejected stings a little. Or a lot.

Have you ever had someone begin a sentence with, "Don't take this personally, but..."? When I hear something like that, I think, How else am I supposed to take it? I suppose a healthy response would be, "Wow, I appreciate you sharing that with me. It just made me a better person, and I'm so grateful for your honesty with me," but to be honest, that's not usually my first reaction. Criticism hurts on a personal level, even when the critic prefaces it with the "don't take this personally" phrase.

Rejection hurts. It does not feel good when you work up the courage to say, "Will you go out with me?" and she says, "Never." Hurt is a natural response when someone rejects us. We all want to be liked. We want everything we do to be approved and even applauded by everyone around us, but that simply isn't realistic. And the reality is that if you have any desire to pursue the dream of God for your life, you will face criticism, rejection, and discouragement. When you have the courage to run after God's will for your life, stepping out and doing things that are out of the norm and pursuing that dream with everything you've got, the difficult truth is, you will be rejected. You will experience criticism.

It is part of the deal.

Life is hard. . . but sometimes you have to put on your big boy pants and move forward. I learned from my football coach back in Tennessee that you still have to play, even when you're hurt. I once heard a Pastor say, "You will gain my respect the moment you can cry all the way to church, preach faith in God, and cry all the way home."

Sometimes you have to play hurt.

It's important to keep playing, to keep going, to press on—especially in the depths of our disappointments. What is hurtful can become extremely harmful if we don't have

God's perspective. "Deferred hope makes the heart sick," according to the old Proverb, "but fulfilled longing is a tree of life" (Proverbs 13:12). The object of your hope is what is important here, and longing for God's perspective is life-giving. There is a danger in not having God's perspective when facing discouragement. Without God's perspective, disappointment can become damaging and causes us to retreat from the dream God has for us.

God is not in the business of taking all the pain away when we are rejected and criticized, because that pain is a reality of the world. Part of the process is gaining a correct perspective. Knowing God's perspective and keeping it in mind is integral in overcoming the hurt that could otherwise derail us from God's dream for our lives.

CHAPTER NINE

WHAT ARE YOU FOR?

The Apostle Paul, who wrote over half of the New Testament, was no stranger to the idea of keeping God's perspective in the face of difficulty. Although he experienced great struggles, a look at his life reveals that somehow in the midst of his pain Paul's purpose was unthwarted. He never retreated from God's dream for him. In the middle of his deepest discouragement, Paul kept his eyes on Jesus.

Paul understood that the moment we allow the criticism of others to stop us, we hand the keys of our dreams over to the critic. The moment you realize, *God is really leading me to step out in faith in this area . . . or, God is really leading me to end this relationship . . . or, God is really leading me to pursue this career. . but I'm worried about what (you fill in the blank) will think,* is the moment the critic wins and gets the keys to your life. God wants you to live free from that kind of oppression, in a place where He is big and the opinions of others are small.

Edward T. Welch's book *When People are Big and God is Small* explains that when we make people big, God and His purposes become small, but when we make God big in our lives, His will and His purposes become the main thing we pursue. If you are going to be able to live the dream and face criticism with success, it'll be because you have made God big in your life.

Paul writes about his experiences on the island of Malta:

> *Once safely on shore, we found out that the island was called Malta. The islanders showed us unusual kindness. They built a fire and welcomed us all because it was raining and cold. Paul gathered a pile of brushwood and, as he put it on the fire, a viper, driven out by the heat, fastened itself on his hand. When the islanders saw the snake hanging from his hand, they said to each other, "This man must be a murderer; for though he escaped from the sea, Justice has not allowed him to live." But Paul shook the snake off into the fire and suffered no ill effects. The people expected him to swell up or suddenly fall dead; but after waiting a long time and seeing nothing unusual happen to him, they changed their minds and said he was a god. There was an estate nearby that belonged to Publius, the chief official of the island. He welcomed us to his home and for three days entertained us hos-*

pitably. His father was sick in bed, suffering from fever and dysentery. Paul went in to see him. After prayer, he placed his hands on him and healed him. When this had happened, the rest of the sick on the island came and were cured. They honored us in many ways; and when we were ready to sail, they furnished us with the supplies we needed.

Acts 28:1-10

Paul is a prisoner, in the custody of a Roman Centurion guard, on a ship headed for Rome for his trial. The ship, carrying 276 people, is caught in very rough seas and then wrecks on Malta, where the islanders greet them with "unusual kindness." The ship's passengers are wet, cold, traumatized from the ship wreck, possibly injured and on the verge of getting sick, and these islanders welcome them and build a fire for them. Paul, who is deep in the process of being shaped by God, is active to do what is in front of him. And what is in front of him is to gather firewood. Practical Paul starts gathering firewood to help these people get warm and dry. When he throws some wood on the fire, the heat drives out a poisonous snake, which bites him.

This is a bad day.

Paul has been imprisoned, shipwrecked, and now a snake is biting him. So he does what any superhero would do: he calmly shakes the snake off, slinging it into the fire.

And a very human thing happens to the islanders: Having shown unusual kindness to Paul and the others, they suddenly change their tune. "He's a murderer!" they begin to say. "I knew it," some whisper. "I saw it in his eyes when he got off the boat."

This is not unlike the way many of us respond in our flesh when someone makes a poor choice or experiences misfortune. What begins as love and acceptance, and even a willingness to help in a tough time, quickly turns to, "I knew it. I didn't trust him from the start." Let me interject this: I think Christians are far too skilled at kicking hard when someone is down. We are often quick to add a swift punch: "I just had a feeling about him. He's getting what he deserves now."

Here's the problem: if we were to get what we deserve, we would all be in big trouble.

Can we decide that we're going to be for healing and restoring people rather than gloating at what they deserve? Can you and I decide we are going to be *for* people, for *loving* people, and for *helping* people?

When people are struggling, we will not stand back and pass judgment, but come to their rescue.

Rather than spewing our own venom at people or about people who have been bitten by snakes, we will seek them out, suck the poison from their wounds and spit it out. Let's just determine this: we will be *for people*!

Because Jesus certainly was.

Back to our story: Paul has shaken the snake from his

hand and the once-kind islanders have turned against him. Rather than helping, they watch and wait for him to die from the snake's venom.

But nothing happens.

Paul is fine.

When the islanders see that he doesn't die, Paul suddenly goes from "murderer" to "god" in their perception.

You simply cannot live your life according to public opinion. If you're going to live God's dream for your life, you must learn to live according to one opinion only: Gods. Public opinion is fickle.

Paul goes from being perceived as a victim needing help, to a murderer, to a god. The once again hospitable islanders bring him to their chief official, who invites him into his home. For three days, he wines and dines Paul. If you know anything about Paul, you know that everywhere he went, he went straight to telling the story of Jesus. Paul would present the Gospel message in every conversation he had: Jesus died; He was buried; He rose again three days later; He can give you forgiveness of sins; He can change your life. Paul simply cut to the chase, with every audience and every chance he had. I have no doubt that during those three days he shared stories of God's greatness and love with the island chief's family.

The official then asks Paul to pray for his ailing father. He had obviously seen power in the life of Paul; why else would he ask this of a stranger? Paul prays for this man's father and the father is miraculously healed. The entire island gets wind of this and they all show up! Everyone on the island who is sick comes to Paul for prayer, and the entire island is cured of its illnesses.

What if Paul had decided to retaliate the moment the islanders turned on him and called him a murderer? Insults and rejections are as difficult to shake off as a viper sometimes. Pithy sayings like, "I'm rubber and you're glue—your words bounce off me and stick to you" are helpful for putting on a brave face, but false. Painful words don't bounce off you.

They have the power to hurt you.

Paul had been through imprisonment and shipwreck—a pretty rough day already—when the islanders began to say those things. So, what if Paul had chosen to sit on the beach and sulk alone under the watchful eye of his Centurion until they fixed the boat and set sail again?

What if Paul had gone onto Facebook and blown it up about how much he hated the island?

Paul would never have made it onto the chief official's radar, let alone into his home.

The chief official would not have seen something in the life of Paul that he admired.

The official would not have asked for prayer for his dad.

Paul would have missed the opportunity to pray and see him healed.

The rest of the island would not have shown up to ask for

prayer and the entire island would not have been healed of their illnesses. If none of that had happened, it follows that the Name of Jesus would never have been lifted up and Paul would not have intersected with these people's lives to give them a picture of the greatness of God.

Paul could have missed all of that, had he let rejection redirect him. But he believed God had some reason for bringing him there. Paul knew with everything in him that God had a purpose for him, that he had the power of God inside of him, and that he had the opportunity to bring a message of life change to the islanders.

And that is exactly what he did.

CHAPTER TEN

HAVING GOD'S PERSPECTIVE

So how did Paul do it? How did he refrain from reacting to being called murderer? These people didn't know him. He had just shown up on the shore. They hadn't hung out with him. They didn't know his heart or his character or his passions or his background. They didn't know that he, in fact, used to be a murderer—of Christians. They didn't know any of that.

I think the answer to Paul's response is found in Philippians 1:21, where he wrote, "For me to live is Christ and to die is gain."

In other words, for me to live in this life, it's all about Jesus, and for me to die, it's all about Jesus. Period.

Whether I live or die, it's all about Jesus.

I live for His Name.

I live for His opinion.

I live for His glory.

I live for His pleasure.

I don't live for the opinions of anyone else.

For me to live is Christ. Everything I have, everything I am, is completely surrendered. I'm dead to all this stuff that seeks to distract and entangle me, and I'm completely alive to Christ.

It is a strange phenomenon when people attend a funeral and tell the family, "She looks really good," or "He looks so peaceful." That doesn't make any sense to me. And you'll notice the deceased never, ever looks up at you and says, "Thanks." My philosophy is, if I look good, tell me now! I want to be able to hear you say it. If you want to send me flowers, send them now (I prefer gift cards, actually). If you wait until I'm dead to say nice things about me or send me gifts, I can't use them. I'm dead. They will make no impact on me whatsoever.

Paul said, "For me to live is Christ." Nothing else. So when people looked at him and said, "He must be a murderer," it was like they were talking about a dead man, and it didn't affect him—because for him, to live was Christ. Period.

Paul had decided he was going to make Jesus greater in his life so all he could see was Jesus. And the result of making Jesus greater in Paul's life was profound: When he was attacked, when he experienced rejection, when he was told "no," when he was called a murderer . . .

He was unfazed.

Dead men don't retaliate; they don't say, "I can't believe you said that about me."

Paul saw everything through this perspective: "I'm dead. For me to live is Christ alone." And that's it. He had made God really big in his life, which made everything else seem really small.

When I get a picture of how great God is in my life, out of that flows a heart of worship for Him greater than my fear or insecurity. It means I get such a picture of how merciful God has been to me, and what He has saved me from, that everything else pales by comparison.

The book of Isaiah says that God holds all the oceans in the divot of His hand. All the oceans on the globe fit right there in God's palm. If I could just ponder that for a moment, it would give me an inkling of how great God is, and it would make everything else seem extremely small. The fear of God gives me so much perspective on God's greatness that all I can do is respond in worship to him. I can't respond in anger or bitterness, because I want to honor God. My heart is to worship Him in all that I do.

Because He is so big, and everything else is really small.

CHAPTER ELEVEN

VALUE, HONOR, AND FEAR

How do we practically live a life of making God really big and making everything else in our lives really small? .

As you pursue God's dream for you, you must value the right opinions. This doesn't mean you ignore all feedback, saying, "I don't care what anybody thinks; I'm just going to do my thing." It doesn't mean you should put "yes men" around you who never speak difficult truth into your life. I am saying value the right opinions.

I have heard it said that there is usefulness in all criticism. I'm sure there's also an earthly use for maggots, but I don't eat them. The fact that someone voices an opinion about your life does not mean you have to pay attention—but you must pay attention to the people who care about you and have been invited to share.

Listening to the people God has placed to speak truth into your life means surrounding yourself with godly people who love you, and love Jesus even more. That kind of person will speak truths, even hard things, but they'll do it when you need to hear those things, because they love you and they love God.

There is a Proverb that says the wounds of a friend can be trusted. You should have godly people in your life who are willing to wound you with the truth if necessary. You should have men and women in your life like the college professor I had, who sat me down at lunch one day and said, "Here are four or five things I see in you that will hold you back from all that God wants to do in your life." He went on to tell me, "You have a very charismatic personality, but I think you're manipulative. I think you're insecure . . ." And he said a few other things I will never forget. But he was a friend, and I knew I could trust the wounds of a friend. You should value the opinions of godly people who will speak truth into your life.

There are people who want to speak truth into your life for the purpose of pulling God's potential out of you, while a critic wants to speak harsh things into your life for the purpose of destroying you. There's a big difference.

If you're going to make God really big, you have to value the right opinions because they will constantly point you to Him. These opinions will challenge you to be more surrendered to Him and to allow certain areas of your life to be consumed with Him. They will not derail you from God's dream for you life, but rather catapult you toward it.

Live with a perspective like Paul's by letting Jesus be your defender. Remember that Paul said, "For me to live is Christ and to die is gain." This means my life is all about Him. Don't waste your time trying to defend yourself or change what others think of you. If you spend your time running after all the no answers, trying to turn them into "yeses," you will rob yourself of the time God wants you to spend pursuing your dream. Keep your eyes focused on what Jesus has called you to do and let Him be your defender.

Will you pray with me? I believe that as you read this today, God may be speaking to you; God may be wanting to break the fear of man, as Proverbs calls it, in which we make choices based on the opinions of others instead of on the opinion of God. I want to pray for you today if you're in that place. Have you avoided a conversation because you're afraid of what they'll think? Have you postponed ending a relationship because you're afraid of what they'll think? Have you stepped away from an opportunity because you're afraid of what they'll think? Are you trapped by the opinions of others and desire to be set free? If that's where you are, I pray that God breaks that today, right now, as you read this. I pray this would be the beginning of a journey in which each day you live for the fear of God, that you will be so awestruck and completely in love with God that the small things fade away, the opinions of others become infinitesimal in your perspective, and nothing stands in the way of your God-given destiny. I pray the things that have been blocking the door between you and God's dream for your life will disappear as He becomes bigger and more awesome to you and you will step through that door, filled with a boldness that comes from knowing you are walking in the will of God, regardless of what others may think. In Jesus' Name, Amen.

CHAPTER TWELVE
HONOR IS THE ANTIDOTE

Have you ever experienced unfair treatment? Maybe it was a promotion you worked hard for but didn't receive. Maybe it was losing your job or experiencing a foreclosure. Was it a friendship that imploded due to circumstances outside of your control? Whatever the situation, we have all experienced events or things in our lives that we felt were unfair.

If anyone knew what it was like to experience the "unfair" side of life, it was Joseph. Betrayed by his own flesh and blood, sold into slavery and now sold again to a man named Potiphar, "unfair" would be putting it lightly. But it is in the moments when life seems unfair that we either embrace the process God is allowing or hijack our destiny. Joseph chose to embrace it!

Embracing the process must be our response as well, because often God is working "behind the scenes." Joseph's move into Potiphar's house was a major step forward; it was, in fact, a practice round for the ultimate destination.

Joseph was about to move into a very powerful position!

We read in the story that "God was with Joseph." He was rejected by his brothers and sold into slavery, but God was with him. This may seem a bit confusing or even contradictory because we often assume God being with us means life on easy street. But that is not reality. Remember, God will never create a life for you that will render Him useless.

It is especially in the difficult times of our lives that God is working on our behalf as well as working in us. God was with Joseph, and when God is with you, the favor of God resting on your life will be evident to those around you.

It was God's favor in Joseph's life that attracted the attention of his new master, Potiphar. Potiphar was in the service of the Pharaoh, the highest official in the land. Historians believe Potiphar was the chief executioner, a man with great authority. In other words, he had the power to make Joseph's life wonderful or to make it a living hell. Because of God's favor, Joseph experienced success in everything he did. So Potiphar put him over everything in his house, and as a result, God blessed everything Potiphar had.

For the first time in his life, Joseph had power, respect, position, and title.

Along with those things came temptation.

Potiphar's wife took notice of Joseph. She made sexual advances toward him, but Joseph, being full of integrity, refused on the grounds of honor.

Joseph honored both God and Potiphar by refusing to

give in to the temptation of Potiphar's wife. "How could I dishonor my master," he asked, "and how could I dishonor God by sinning against Him?"

Honor is how we make God big in our lives; it's how we keep our focus on Jesus and minimize the things in our lives that try to take our eyes off of Him. Showing honor mutes the critic, refuses rejection, and resists temptation. It's how we take back the keys to the dream God wants us to live. Honor is the antidote.

Joseph could have given in to the temptation and no one would have ever known. It might have even made Joseph's life easier, as he would have received special treatment and privileges from his boss's wife.

The enemy will offer temptations in an effort to hijack the process and sabotage God's dream for you:

Temptation to forego integrity in order to get ahead.

Temptation to see people as pawns in the game of your success.

Temptation to elevate yourself instead of allowing God to elevate you.

Joseph didn't take the bait but chose honor instead. To honor someone is to treat them as uncommon, to esteem them, to anticipate their needs. Honor is the antidote to the temptation you will face, and the test you must pass in order to graduate to the next level.

Perhaps you are in a situation with some difficult people right now, and you are thinking, *These people don't deserve my honor.*

They may not deserve your respect, but everyone deserves your honor. Respect is earned; honor is given. If I'm going to honor God, I'm going to honor others.

I can't be bitter toward someone I'm honoring; honor becomes the antidote to a bitter heart.

I won't stay angry with someone I honor; honor becomes the antidote to anger.

I can't live disconnected from someone and still honor God; honor is the antidote to apathy.

I won't betray someone to whom I am trying to show honor; honor is the antidote to temptation.

How do you *do* honor?

One practical tool that has helped me is keeping a heart of prayer. It's much easier to honor someone, and to refrain from retaliation, when you are praying for the one who hurt you.

An individual wrote a blog post about me a few years ago, criticizing me as a "spiky haired, blue jeans-wearing Pastor." He was criticizing something he thought he understood about me and didn't like. I didn't even know this person, and he didn't know me, but he criticized me publicly.

I could have been offended. I could have quickly typed up a sarcastic rebuttal and published a blog post of my own in response. But God showed me that I needed to stop and pray blessings over the one who had offended me. Now don't get me wrong—I didn't feel much like doing that at first, but I have learned not to go by my feelings when it comes to obeying God.

We honor those who dishonor us by praying for them: "God, I pray you bless that person. I pray you will cause the sun to shine on him. I pray you cause favor to flow in his life. I pray you will cause his family to be strong and have victory and success."

I have found that if I try to pray every good thing I can possibly think for the person who has wounded me, my heart slowly begins to turn. In my willingness to please God, after a few words in prayer I really begin to mean it, and in those moments, I give honor. I think this is why Jesus said we should pray for those who persecute us—because through prayer, God has the power to turn our hearts.

My heart needs to be turned when it is hurt. My heart often wants to retaliate, but prayer softens me. It has become the key to my ability to show honor, especially in situations in which I feel honor isn't due.

Honoring others empowers you to take back the keys to your dream. Honor opens doors you could never open on your own. Honor will give you an audience with individuals you would otherwise never meet. Honor gives you access.

Honor was the antidote to the temptation Joseph faced.

Day after day, Potiphar's wife tempted Joseph, but each day, out of honor for Potiphar, he refused her propositions. The temptation became stronger as he continued to resist. Sometimes it feels like the more we pursue God's plan, the more temptation tries to break down our resistance. But at the same time our resistance is being challenged, it's also being built.

Temptation doesn't attempt a knockout blow on day one; it seeks to erode resistance little by little. One compromise after another finds us doing things we never dreamed we would do. But honor allows us to stand when temptation tries to overthrow our resistance. We get stronger the more we resist - it's the power of the process and it's the purpose of the preparation.

The enemy will no doubt attempt to sabotage your dream by luring you to a tradeoff.

Maybe it will be trading integrity for immediate advancement.

Or trading a great life for a good life.

Or trading God's promotion for self-promotion.

Or trading faith in God for self-reliance.

The enemy will offer this kind of tradeoff in an effort to hijack the process and derail God's dream for you. And when we fall to these temptations, we sabotage the fulfillment of God's dream for our lives. We begin to think working for Potiphar isn't such a bad thing after all, when God has so much more.

Those who refuse to take the tradeoff will live their dreams.

Those people change the world.

CHAPTER THIRTEEN

THE POWER OF THE PROCESS

Joseph didn't take the bait, but responded with honor.

However, Joseph didn't form integrity in that moment--it was already formed in him. Pressure simply showed the true character of Joseph and gave him an opportunity to prove himself trustworthy. You don't form integrity in the moment of temptation. Your character is merely revealed in those moments.

One day Potiphar's wife found Joseph alone in the house and made another advance—this time, grabbing him and demanding he go to bed with her. Once again acting with honor and integrity, Joseph responded by running (always the best response to temptation!) and leaving his outer garment in her hand. Potiphar's wife, rejected and resentful, accused Joseph of attacking her, using his garment as proof. Potiphar, angry at Joseph's alleged betrayal, had Joseph thrown in Pharaoh's jail.

So honor landed Joseph in jail and his life once again seemed destroyed. Maybe you're thinking, *If this is where honor takes you, then count me out!* But in reality, Joseph's honor was not only the antidote to his temptation but also the agent for his promotion. What Joseph didn't know was that God was again relocating him in order to promote him to the next level. Prison would become the green room--the holding room before God placed Joseph on the main stage.

Joseph's entire experience to this point could have caused him to stop, to step out of the process, and to question if his dream was even from God. But Joseph had the correct perspective. He allowed his employment at Potiphar's house to become a practice ground for what lay ahead. He did not allow Potiphar's house to become his destination, but rather an opportunity to practice for his next level. Joseph didn't let his position determine his passion. He learned to practice.

It may be that you are looking for a major breakthrough, a spotlight opportunity, or for someone to use his or her platform to propel your dream. Instead, God will open up doors of opportunity for you to practice and hone your gift.

The crowd may not be large.

The opportunity may not feel significant.

But you will have room to practice.

The summer before my senior year of high school, God gave me a burden for my peers, and I decided to plan an outreach event. I created the marketing pieces, recruited a team to help me plan the event, and assigned myself as the guest speaker. (When you're running the event you can make that decision.)

I just knew there would be a line of people at the door, waiting to get into this event.

To my dismay, that wasn't the situation at all. No more than 15 people showed up. But at the age of seventeen, I gave the best sermon I could come up with, and six minutes later I closed with prayer. It wasn't what I had dreamed it would be, but it allowed me to practice—both practically and spiritually. God taught me something that day: when He is with me, nothing is a failure or a waste of time, no matter how it looks on the surface. I'm thoroughly convinced I have the privilege of speaking to thousands of people every weekend at our church today because I was willing to practice then for what God had planned for me now.

This is true all the way through the story: Joseph knew God's character was constant, even when the circumstances appeared bleak. He was not dependent on what his situation was, but on who he knew God to be.

Though Joseph had a change in condition, he had not changed in spirit.

Though separated from his earthly father, he was not separated from his Heavenly Father.

Though he was in the house of someone far from God, he continued to be a dependent of the one true God.

Joseph had a never quit mentality, even when his dream

seemed to be dead, his life seemed to be coming to an end, and his own family had rejected him. God honored Joseph, and he began to see the light at the end of the tunnel. He began to experience the favor of God in his life.

Too many people stop short of this moment—they don't push through and continue to do the right thing when they experience difficulty. They quit, mere moments before their breakthrough. Joseph didn't quit—he pressed in and refused to miss what God wanted to do in his life. And you also must have a never quit mentality if you're going to live the dream.

You can't allow fear or failure to cause you to quit.

You can't allow a lack of resources to cause you to quit.

You can't allow rejection to cause you to quit.

You can't allow insecurities to cause you to quit.

And you can't allow the critics to cause you to quit.

You have to adopt the mentality of Joseph—the mentality of Winston Churchill's famous 1941 speech: "Never give in. Never give in. Never, never, never, never—in nothing, great or small, large or petty—never give in." You have come too far; you have prayed too long and believed too much to turn back now.

Could it be that the difficulties you are facing are not the result of God's absence in your life, but rather the fact that He is very much engaged? Often our expectations of how God will work and how God is working are very different. Sometimes in the midst of doing the right thing, you experience bad things . . . and that is exactly what God allows, because He is setting you up to advance to a new level, where the fulfillment of your dream is right around the corner.

If anyone had reason to whine and complain, it was Joseph. If anyone had grounds to ask "why" or to check out, it was Joseph. If anyone had a legitimate reason to claim that life isn't fair, it was Joseph.

But as God shapes our hearts, fairness is not His goal. Fairness is an illegitimate desire that subverts the deeper work God is doing in us.

Our minds and emotions may desire fairness, but God is more concerned about our holiness. God will allow and even create seemingly unfair situations in our lives to renew our hearts. Even during what seemed unfair, God was with Joseph.

And more importantly, God was giving Joseph the strength he would need to persevere.

CHAPTER FOURTEEN
YOUR THINKING IS THE DRIVER

When I was in the first grade I attended a Christian school in South Carolina, and I decided I would take my Hot Wheels cars to class with me one day. I always had tons of Hot Wheels cars because my sisters gave them to me every Christmas. I wanted to take my cars to school with me because I understood something about academics that most elementary teachers don't: first grade is mainly for playing. For me it was playing with Hot Wheels, but really any toy will do. Some people think first grade is for reading and writing and arithmetic. Not so much for me.

I had these cars on my desk, playing with them, and of course the teacher told me to put them away. Now I wasn't an ornery or rebellious kid, but I was mischievous. I put them away as she asked, but knowing what first grade was really about, I soon snuck the cars out from my desk and continued to play with them. Of course, my teacher saw what I was doing, and quickly took the cars away from me. At the end of the day she explained she would be holding my cars hostage until I came back to her with the ransom: a note I was to take home and have my mom or dad sign, letting them know what had taken place.

You might think I would be worried about this, but I wasn't just mischievous, I was smart and I had a brilliant idea. I knew how to spell my mom's last name. It was the same name as mine, and not only did I know how to spell it, I had even had some practice writing it. Now, I didn't know how to spell her first name, but I knew my dad was home and I figured he knew how to spell it. So I went home, went into my room, put the teacher's note down, and started working on it. Meanwhile, my Dad was in his recliner, so I began to execute my plan. I went out to the family room and asked my Dad, "How do you spell Mom's name?"

My Dad answered, "M-Y-R-A."

I said, "Wait one second," so I went back. M—got it. And I came back out. "What's the next letter?" He answered, "Y." And so this pattern continued until in my best first-grade writing I had completely signed my mom's name on this piece of paper. I would return it to the teacher the following day, rescue my toys, and get back to my first-grade education with Hot Wheels.

The following day I brought the note in and boldly handed it to the teacher. The next thing I knew, I found myself in the hallway outside the principal's office. My older sister happened to be walking by at precisely that moment, and asked, "Why are you in trouble?"

I quickly answered, "I saw a fight and they want me to tell them what happened."

So at this point, not only had I forged my mom's name on the paper from my teacher, I had also lied to my sister. And in my mind, somehow I still thought I had the whole thing under control.

The principal invited me into his office, pulled out the note, placed it in front of me on the desk and asked me point blank, "Daniel, did you sign this?" I said, "No. My mom signed it."

The principal pulled out a different document, one with my mom's actual signature on it, and held it out for me to compare it to mine. Pointing at the two signatures, he asked me, "Do these look the same?"

I replied, "Pretty close."

Needless to say, my web of lies finally caught up with me and I got in trouble. I didn't get my Hot Wheels back, and my mom and dad found out what I had done.

Now, to give you a little context, my Dad was a Pastor in the community. And I don't know if you grew up in a home like this, but in my family we all knew if you get in trouble at school, Lord help you, because it's going to be ten times worse when you get home. As a matter of fact, my dad used to have meetings with the principal at the beginning of each year, in which he would say, "You don't paddle them (yes, they still used paddles when I was in elementary school); You call me." And we were always thinking, No—please let the principal paddle us instead!

The thing is, I turned in that forged piece of paper because I believed I was going to get away with it. There was not a second thought in my mind. I was going to walk in, turn in this note with my first-grade cursive on it, tell the teacher my mom had signed it, get my Hot Wheels back, and everything was going to be great. I honestly believed this, and my behavior followed my belief.

This same principle holds true for all of us, no matter what age or stage of life we're in: our beliefs drive our behavior. You don't have to listen to people talk to find out what they really believe. You just have to watch how they live. How we live is the greatest indicator of what we truly believe.

If you want to know what you believe about finances, open your checkbook register and take a look at the record of your behavior. If you want to find out what someone believes about relationships, watch how he or she engages with others and you'll know. What we believe is not revealed in what we say, but in how we live.

Let me give you a very elementary example of this. You know that if a burner on your stove is lit and you put your hand on it, you will get burned. And because you believe that, your behavior follows—you simply don't put your hand on lit burners.

However, you didn't come out of the womb knowing not to touch a hot stove. In fact, lit burners on the stove in my house light up in a pretty red glow that actually drew my kids like moths to a flame when they were babies. They would see that red glowing burner and reach for it, wanting to touch it. They had no idea how badly it could hurt them.

But somewhere along the way, either through our parents' instruction or through a horrible experience, we find out that a hot stove will burn us and we replace our desire to touch the hot burner with a new belief—we shouldn't touch it because it will hurt us. Our belief drives our behavior.

Sundays at our church could not be pulled off without the army of volunteers who love what they do and do it with passion. One Sunday recently, a member of our parking team reminded me of a story we try to remember whenever we look at our systems and structures: A woman is cooking dinner for her family, and as she is cooking, her child asks why she is cutting the ends off the ham. She calls her mom and asks, "Mom, why do we always cut the ends off of the ham when we cook it?" Her mother answers, "I don't know. You'll have to ask your grandmother." So the woman calls her grandmother to ask the same question, and is amazed to hear the answers: "Well, we didn't have a pan that was big enough for the ham so we always cut the ends off so it would fit."

It sounds crazy, but the truth is, some of us live this

way. We go through the motions, doing things a certain way without even knowing the reason. We don't question it, but somewhere along the line we just end up thinking a certain way and believing certain things. And we behave accordingly.

There comes a moment in life when we have a change in our thinking, and our thinking has to change in order for our behavior to change. This is why Paul said in Romans 12:2 that we are to be transformed. That word transformed comes from the word metamorphosis. It's what happens to a caterpillar: it goes into the cocoon as one thing and comes out completely different.

Completely new.

That's what Paul is talking about when he says, "transformed." When we place our faith in Jesus and give our lives to Him, we know our destiny is Heaven, but it doesn't stop there. With God's help, we continue to be completely transformed. It's a process—a journey we're all on, each on different legs of the journey. Paul must have known that what we believe drives how we live on this journey, because he says we can be transformed by the renewing of our minds.

And with what do I renew my mind?

I renew it with truth.

Jesus said, "You will know the truth, and the truth will set you free (John 8:32)." Truth renews your mind, and as your mind is renewed, the way you live begins to change.

We can practice behavior modification, but it only lasts

for a season. Around the first week of January, the parking lot at the gym I belong to will be packed, and I'll lose my front row parking spot that I usually have in September and October. Every January, as a New Year's resolution, many commit to getting in shape. But by about January 15th, I'll get my parking spot back.

Behavior modification is short lived.

It might stick longer for some people, and their behavior will be somewhat modified. We can attempt that, but it is almost always temporary. There has to come a time in our lives when we renew our minds, and our behavior will follow.

Maybe this is your story. You realized Jesus died for you, was buried and rose again three days later, and you placed your faith in Him. However, there are some areas in this journey of knowing Jesus where you still feel stuck.

That's been my experience, too. There are some areas of my life in which I feel like I just can't get traction. I feel like I just can't get past a certain mark. I really want to advance in my walk with God. I want to know Him better and be more in love with Him. I want to live a life that pleases Him more, but time after time I make a commitment to change a certain behavior, and then fall off the wagon.

We don't find traction in those instances because we are attempting to follow Jesus with an old mindset. Until you believe what God says to believe, you will remain on the treadmill of trying to change your behavior without having changed your thinking. Like a hamster on a wheel, you just keep running without getting anywhere because without changing your thinking, you will never see lasting change in your behavior.

Your thinking is the driver.

CHAPTER FIFTEEN

A NEW WAY OF THINKING

If we really want to be transformed, we need to change our thinking and renew our minds by ripping out some bad thinking and replacing it with the Word of God.

John, one of the disciples who walked most closely with Jesus while He was here on the earth writes about how renewed thinking led to serious transformation:

> *Some time after this, Jesus crossed to the far shore of the Sea of Galilee, that is the sea of Tiberius, and a great crowd of people followed him because they saw the miraculous signs he performed on the sick. Then Jesus went up on a mountainside and sat down with his disciples. The Jewish Passover feast was near.*
>
> John 6:1-4

As this story begins, we find Jesus has been out doing what Jesus does. He has been healing people, teaching people, ministering to people; He has had crowds of thousands of people following him. So He goes up on a mountainside, sits down with his disciples, and thousands of people follow in the hopes of learning from Him. They don't even know what He's going to do on that mountain.

Is He going to teach?

Is He going to pray?

Is He going to perform miracles?

What's He going to do?

Thousands of people come, just to find out.

Now in this story, 5,000 men followed Jesus up on that mountainside. That's just the men; even if only half of those guys are married and have kids, there are 10,000 . . . 15,000 . . . 20,000 . . . possibly 30,000 people on this mountainside, following Jesus, wondering what He will do next.

When Jesus looked up and saw a great crowd coming toward Him, He said to Philip, "Where shall we buy bread for these people to eat?" He asked this only to test him, for He already had in mind what He was going to do. Philip answered Him, "Eight months' wages would not buy enough bread for each one to have a little bite."

John 6:5-7

If you will look around, you'll often find that God is setting you up to teach you something. The situation you're in right now could very well be a teachable moment. When faced with a task that seems unattainable, a situation that seems unsolvable, or an obstacle that seems insurmountable, stop for a moment. Don't fight it, because it could be that God is trying to teach you something in the middle of all of it—something you need to know for the next leg of your journey.

Jesus looks at Philip and says, "What are we going to feed these people?" Jesus already knew what He was going to do. He was setting His disciples up to teach them something.

Philip, living and speaking out what he believes, says, "It would take eight months' wages to feed this many people."

In other words, "Are you kidding me? There is no way we are going to be able to feed all of these people!"

Philip's belief, as evidenced by his words, is that the only way to meet the insurmountable need in front of him is to save and to work and to scrape together and hold together until we've got enough money, and then go buy some food.

Philip's thinking is understandable: *There is a need, it's too much, and there's no way we could ever meet it. The only solution is to work and work and save and save, and then—maybe—we'll be able to meet the need. Jesus, that's the only solution we've got.*

Aren't we just like Philip sometimes? We face situations

in which the need seems greater than our resources. Have you ever experienced the realization in which your need is much greater than your available resource? I'm not just talking about finances. I'm talking about relationships. I'm talking about emotions. I'm talking about situations in which there is a deficit in your life and your resources are far less than what you need. Have you ever been there? Sometimes the deficit is all we can see.

That's all Philip can see.

And Jesus is about to shift his thinking.

Another of the disciples, Andrew, volunteers some information. He has found a boy in the crowd who has five small barley loaves and two fish. At least Andrew is being resourceful, but his thinking is still limited.

"How far will they go among so many?" he asked.

It's a legitimate question.

He's got five pieces of bread and two fish. Even if they were big fish, they still wouldn't be enough to feed thousands of people.

> *Jesus said, "Have the people sit down." There was plenty of grass in that place, and they sat down (about 5,000 men were there.) Jesus then took the loaves, gave thanks, and distributed to those who were seated as much as they wanted. He did the same with the fish. When they had all had enough to eat, He said to the disciples, "Gather the pieces*

that are left over. Let nothing be wasted."

John 6:10-12

So they started with five barley loaves, two fish, and a certain mindset. When everyone had eaten all they wanted to eat, the disciples found they had twelve baskets full of the remaining pieces.

And they had a new way of thinking.

CHAPTER SIXTEEN

GIVE WHAT YOU'VE GOT

Jesus gave His disciples a new way of thinking by teaching them to give what you've got. He changed their thinking about the subject of generosity, and I believe we need to renew our thinking about this subject, as well. Jesus desires for His Church to be a radically generous bunch of people. I'm not just talking about finances. I'm talking about everything we do. I'm talking about being radically generous in encouraging others.

In loving people—even those who are unlike us.

In showing compassion to people.

In offering hope to the world.

We should be radically generous people because God is a radically generous God, and we are created in His image. As image-bearers of God, it is our job to reflect the nature and the character of God. In other words, we are like walking mirrors on this earth, reflecting God to the world around us.

John quotes Jesus as telling us what kind of giver God is: "For God so loved the world that He gave His one and only Son, that whoever believes in Him shall not perish but have eternal life."

Because of His radically generous love for the world, God radically, generously, *gave* His only Son. Those of us who have placed our faith in Jesus are the recipients of that love. Shouldn't we then be radically generous people?

Shouldn't we be generous in offering forgiveness?

Shouldn't we be generous in loving people?

Shouldn't we be generous in offering restoration to people?

Shouldn't we be generous in offering healing to people?

Shouldn't we be the most generous people on the planet?

Shouldn't the world look at the Church and say, "Wow, they don't just have their hand out. They're always giving a hand up because they're generous to everyone." God has taught us to be a radically generous bunch of people, to be an over-the-top, double-for-your-trouble kind of people.

Back to our story of loaves and fish from the last chapter: When it came to feeding thousands of people, the disciples saw the only solution as *work, work, work, save, save, save, and then purchase some bread.*

The little boy in the story had a different thought. He brought his five loaves and two fish to Jesus. His actions portray a different thought: *give what I have to Jesus and see what Jesus can do with it attitude.*

He just gave Jesus what he had.

It wasn't much. It was five pieces of bread and two fish. It wouldn't make a dent in the hunger of 5,000 people. One grown man could eat that by himself and still be hungry. But for some reason, the boy walked up to one of the disciples and said, "I've got this and I'm willing to give what I've got."

Even though the need in your life may seem insurmountable, Jesus wants to teach you to give what you've got.

Jesus wants you to come to a place where you don't look at your situation and say, "Wow, the need is insurmountable, so I'm just going to hang on tightly to what I have. I'm going to scrimp and save and protect my own interests, and I'm not going to give any of it away because my own need is so great, and the economy is horrible, and I am afraid."

We can add a little bit here and there to the little bit we've got. But if we'll put it in the hands of Jesus, He doesn't just add to it. He multiplies it. He can take five barley loaves and two fish and, in an instant, turn it into a feast for thousands with 12 baskets to spare.

But we must be willing to give what we've got.

Does our behavior really reflect a belief that if we'll give our little to Jesus, He can make a whole lot out of it? Let's do an inventory. Is there anyone in your life from whom you're withholding forgiveness? Is there someone at your office who you know just needs some encouragement or kind words to get through the day? Is there maybe just a little something you can give that God can multiply into so much more, to meet a huge need for someone else?

If we really believed God could take our little and make a whole lot out of it, we would be willing to give a little bit of encouragement along the way. We would be willing to give a little bit of hope. We would be willing to give a little bit of comfort to someone in need. We'd be willing to give a little bit of our time to listen to someone else's problem. If we really believed God could take our little bit and make something great out of it, we'd be willing to give what we've got.

I'm afraid that in our fast-paced lives, our actions show we really don't believe God can take our little and make a lot out of it. And when our pattern of thinking is wrong, we're going to have wrong behavior.

When we have a pattern of thinking we have lived with for years, we also have certain habits and ways we do life. If we continue to think the way we always have, we will never see our five barley loaves and two fish turn into a feast with 12 baskets left over.

Some of us have people in our lives who already understand the "give what you've got" concept. We look at them and think, *Man, they're so blessed. I don't understand why God keeps blessing them and doesn't bless me.*

I have an idea about those people, that maybe underneath all the blessings we see, there is a radically generous giver. If we've never received in abundance from God, it could be because we've never given in abundance to God.

This is never about what God wants from you.

This isn't even about finances.

This is simply about God wanting you to reflect His nature and His character, which means, among other things, that you are radically generous.

It means you give what you've got.

CHAPTER SEVENTEEN
HOLD ON LOOSELY

I was 17 years old, newly graduated from high school, and ready to go for it when I first left home. I had great parents and a great life, but I was ready to get out there and start on my own course. I wanted to take life by the horns and ride it. So I moved into a three-bedroom apartment with five other guys in Nashville, Tennessee. I found a job at a Wilson Sporting Goods factory. I was set.

Have you ever, while shopping in a sporting goods section, seen a basketball with a box around it? You can see the ball, but it's in a box that can be stacked and displayed in the store. My job at the Wilson factory was to sit by a bin full of basketballs, and each day I would box the whole bin. I would take the cardboard thing out, set it up, stuff the ball in it, close it, and put it in a box to be shipped to Walmart or Target. It was a classy job.

I did that for eight hours a day, while simultaneously

debating an agnostic guy that worked right beside me at his own bin. All day long this guy would talk about how he believed in a higher power but not Jesus, and all day long I would try to convince him that the Jesus of the Bible is real. It was great training for me. We would debate and stuff basketballs all day long, eight hours a day, five days a week.

My next job was a little cushy. I began working for the University I attended. I had a desk job, which was more comfortable than sitting by a bin at the factory, and made for an easier workday.

When I was stuffing basketballs and making 50 cents more per hour than minimum wage, I was faithful to tithe. Giving ten percent of $200.00 a week to my church was not too hard, because it's a tiny bit of money. But when I started working for the University I began to receive a salary. I was thinking, I'm walking in high cotton now. I felt like I'd hit the jackpot. But I knew all of it—the salary, the benefits, all of it—were gifts from God, because God had blessed me with that job in the first place.

You think, *You earned the job—you worked hard—you showed up for work and did well. You earned your salary there.* And you're right, I did work hard; I put my all into it. But I knew everything we have comes from God. James 1:17 says every good and perfect gift comes from the Father above. It is God who gives us the ability to gain wealth.

So when my first paycheck came through on direct deposit, it was a lot more than what I had earned at the factory. Tithing now took a much bigger chunk. And the blessing of my new job and increased salary could have become the very thing that kept me from being faithful and generous.

If you are going to live the dream God has placed inside you, that dream must be resourced. Dreams are costly, and God needs to know He can trust you to hold His blessings with an open hand. When we get our claws into the blessing of God, that blessing can become the very thing that keeps us from receiving all that God wants to give us.

The same principle holds true for organizations. A few years ago, when our church consisted of a couple hundred people, it was easy to take risks. God would ask us to take a bold step—give money away, give to missions, or help plant another church—and it was easy. We didn't have anything. I mean, when all you've got is $2.00, it's easy to say, "Sure, have $2.00." Our Executive Pastor, Jeremy, and I were the only paid staff. We had so few obligations that it was easy to be radically generous.

Jeremy and I could eat all of our meals at McDonald's, Chick-Fil-A, or wherever. We didn't have kids yet, and our wives were brave enough to come along on the journey with us. When I sat down with our leadership team and said, "I heard about this idea of dropping eggs out of a helicopter at Easter and I think we should do it" they may have thought I was crazy, but they agreed. It would take every bit of money we had in the bank, but they said, "Let's do it."

We dropped 10,000 eggs and had 3,500 people show up.

We were giving away flat-screen TVs and other prizes, so parents went bananas getting eggs and tackling kids. But ultimately, we were a church of 200 who ministered to 3500 people in one event. We thought it was the greatest thing ever.

But now we have multiple people on staff. There are thousands in attendance at our church each weekend. There's a lot more at risk. God has blessed us greatly. And sometimes as a leader, I fight the temptation of allowing the blessing of God to become the very thing that causes me to step back, with all that's at stake now, and think, I don't know if we should risk so much.

I don't know if we should take that step of faith.

I don't know if we should be so generous.

Sometimes I find myself wondering, Should we really have given away $140,000 to needy people and missions in the first nine months of this year? Because the blessing of God—the growth that we've experienced—the lives that have been changed—can become the very things that cause me to step back and think, *It's a lot more costly now.*

I have learned that whenever I get to a place in life or in ministry where I hold on too tightly to what God has given me, the flow of His blessing stops immediately. But the moment my hands are open again, the blessings begin to flow. If I'm willing to live life with open hands—to lead this church, manage my personal finances, and raise my children with forgiveness, love, hope, and compassion; to offer healing to people and say, "God, give as much as you can possibly give through me into the lives of other people"—I find that He continues to make me a bigger conduit of His blessing into the lives of others. But the moment I clamp my hands tightly, trying to keep control, is the moment I cap off the flow of blessing in my life.

The reason for this is simple: it's not what God wants from me. It's what He wants for me, and what He wants to do through me. God wants you to live with radical generosity, and not because He's trying to get something from you. God doesn't need a jobs plan or a bailout. He's trying to get something into your hands, because He has this idea that He will raise up an army of people who will be so radically generous that He would be able to give them crazy resources and trust them to give hope, love, peace, compassion, and yes, their finances, to others. And the world will never be the same.

Jesus told us this is true.

He says it like this in Luke 6:38: Give, and it will be given to you. A good measure, pressed down, shaken together and running over, will be poured into your lap. For with the measure you use, it will be measured to you.

Surely this is not so we can hold onto it! It's so we can give again—so we can give more. Then that amount will get pressed down, shaken together, begin to overflow, and be given back to us.

This is not just about your pocketbook. This is about being a radically generous person to everyone around you. Think about it: if you need encouragement today, give encouragement to someone else, because what you give is what you're going to get. If you need hope today, find someone in the middle of your pain who also needs hope. Give them hope and you'll find it coming back to you—pressed down, shaken together, and running over. If you need forgiveness, find all who have offended you and forgive them. Jesus says if you'll do this, God will pour a pressed-down-shaken-together-running-over amount of forgiveness back into your lap. If you need the blessing of God in your life, go bless someone, because what you give is what will come back to you in abundance.

What if we all decided we were going to live that way? What if we said, "God, transform my thinking; I've had a pattern of thinking that is wrong, and I need You to renew my mind." That's hard to do, but what if we actually did it?

What if we said, "God, I want to replace my own pattern with a God-honoring pattern of thinking, so that my behavior reflects You, and You flow out of me"?

What if we replaced our patterns of thinking with a *generous* God kind of thinking, the kind of generosity that led Him to give up His one and only Son? He gave up everything. Our worship team once wrote a song, Overflow, which says, "My heart cannot contain this love that gave up everything." I want that kind of thinking—that kind of generosity—to flow through me and overflow out of me. I want to give with a mentality that God will open the windows of Heaven into my life and allow me to be His overflow into the lives of those around me.

Don't get me wrong. This isn't about "give God a dollar and He'll give you a hundred." God is not our genie in a bottle. He is God, the Creator of the Universe. If He wanted your money, He would direct deposit it into His account right now. This is about the fact that God seems to bless certain activities. Certain activities trigger faith, and faith is what pleases God, which ultimately moves the hand of God in our lives.

What if we all actually did this? How do you think it would change your work environment if you decided to sow faith?

To sow encouragement?

To show appreciation?

To sow love into the lives of those who are really difficult?

How would this change the landscape of your community?

How would your radically generous behavior change your world and begin to change everything for you?

Could you be a part of the solution to homelessness in your community? Could you be a part of providing education and training, of helping people get on their feet? Does it sound crazy to even think this is a possibility?

I started thinking beyond that: What if all of us who call ourselves Christians decided we would be generous in encouragement, and love, and forgiveness, and hope? I believe it would radically change the landscape of our society. Think about it: there must be thousands, maybe tens of thousands of people who attend church regularly. What if every one of them left church each week and infected their communities with generosity? The world would never be the same.

You may be thinking, this sounds great, but how do I rally everyone around me to a goal like that?

You can't.

All you can be responsible for is you. So why not determine in your heart that you will be responsible for you today by changing your thinking? Ask God to renew your mind as it relates to generosity so your behavior will be transformed, and the world around you will know the goodness of God through you.

This isn't about getting something from God. It's about being a funnel for the blessing of God in the lives of those around you. If you do this as you live out the dream God has placed in your heart, buckle your seat belt. I believe God will resource your dream on a level you never dreamed possible.

CHAPTER EIGHTEEN

BEFORE A BREAKTHROUGH

Have you ever felt like you have taken three steps forward only to take twenty steps back? This had to be how Joseph felt. Having been rejected by his family and sold into slavery, he experienced a breakthrough in finding favor at Potiphar's house, only to then be falsely accused and find himself back in prison.

Talk about moving backwards!

These are the moments in which our grit is tested. Do we have the tenacity, the discipline, and the fortitude to keep moving forward? It takes a certain level of mental and emotional sturdiness to keep pressing in when progress seems elusive. I believe the character created in such moments allows us to carry the weight of being used greatly.

When we act justly and injustice befalls us, strength is forged and our true motives come to light. When we don't get what we think we're entitled to, the spotlight shines on the true intentions of our hearts. It's in those moments that the true testing of the soul takes place.

Joseph was in prison. but this was no ordinary prison. It was the place where the King's prisoners were kept. If there were a prison to be in, this was the one (sarcasm intended). Can you imagine how he must have felt, again?

Alone.

Abandoned.

Unfairly treated.

Retracing in his mind all the events that had led up to that moment.

Joseph was entering the final stage of preparation before God would move him to the palace—but the road from Potiphar's house to the palace went through a prison.

And as God shapes you on your journey, there could be a prison moment in which your motives will be tested. There could be a season in which you feel lost, abandoned, rejected, even tempted to give up the dream. In that instant you must answer the question: *Who are you doing this for?*

When you are living your dream, who will get the glory?

Are you living for the glory of yourself—with all the attention focused on you and your accomplishments? Are you the main character, the hero of your story?

Or have you purposed in your heart to live for something greater? Is the glory of God your highest pursuit? Is your motive that this small part you are playing would simply join in the storyline that directs all of creation for time and eternity to the greatness of God—even if your part in the story means your prison season doesn't end?

Is God's glory, in and through your own difficulty, worth it?

It was for Joseph.

We read in the story that God was with Joseph in prison. God never expected Joseph to walk his journey alone and He doesn't expect you to walk yours alone.

Once again, the reality of Joseph's favor with God attracted additional favor from people. Favor is the expression of God's grace in order to accomplish God's purpose for His glory and our good. No matter the situation, Joseph continued to rise to the top. Favor works like that.

Favor opens doors you can't open on your own.

Favor gives you access you would not otherwise have.

Favor ain't fair. (I know that's not good grammar but it's true nonetheless.)

Joseph found favor with the prison warden. This took place because Joseph was living out "who" he was and "whose" he was. He knew he was a follower of God. He was determined not to turn his back on the One who had given him the dream.

Joseph's character and conduct were not affected by his circumstances; they were the direct result of a dependence on God that began in the cistern in which his brothers had thrown him. The weight of the responsibility Joseph would one day carry was being tested by the weight of the mistreatment he experienced. The truth of Joseph's heart would come out in the prison. Would his life be marked by the pursuit of a dream, or by a heart so molded in God's hand that it had one motive, one pursuit: the glory of God?

The warden put Joseph in charge of the entire prison. This gave Joseph authority but also kept him under authority. He was responsible for managing the inmates, but he reported directly to the warden. Joseph knew that to have authority you must submit to authority.

A very important lesson on the path to greatness is this: until you are willing to get under what God puts over you, you will never be over what God wants to place under you. This isn't a popular subject when the flow of culture says to be your own person, resist authority, and question everything. You can choose to resist the spiritual, civil, family, or even career authority structures in your life, but understand that when you do that, you remove yourself from the blessing of God and the potential to be elevated by God.

God blesses and elevates through authority structures. Think about it: the only person in your work environment who can bless you with a raise or elevate you with a promotion is the person in authority over you. Why? Because blessing and favor flow through lines of authority!

During Joseph's time as an inmate, the Pharaoh became angry with his cup-bearer and his chief baker and threw them both in prison. The cup-bearer was in charge of the royal vineyards and cellars—he most likely had hundreds of people working under his leadership. The chief baker was also in a position of authority, responsible for everything related to providing and serving food for the royal table.

These two individuals had great access to the Pharaoh, which meant they had great status in the kingdom. However, for some reason the Pharaoh became angry and threw them both in the prison in which Joseph now lived and worked.

Joseph couldn't have known his life had just intersected with someone who would later open the door to his dream. But he cared for these prisoners anyway. Joseph valued people, no matter their status or circumstances. He valued those who were in front of him. Joseph didn't need a platform. He didn't need a title. He didn't even need freedom to value the people around him. Joseph was simply being who God wanted him to be, regardless of the situation. This was a man who could be entrusted with the great things God had for him.

While under Joseph's care, both the cup-bearer and the baker have dreams they can't understand:

> *While they were in prison, Pharaoh's cup-bearer and baker each had a dream one night, and each dream had its own meaning. When Joseph saw them the next morning, he noticed that they both looked upset. "Why do you look so worried today?" he asked them. And they replied, "We*

both had dreams last night, but no one can tell us what they mean." "Interpreting dreams is God's business," Joseph replied. "Go ahead and tell me your dreams." So the chief Cup-bearer told Joseph his dream first. "In my dream," he said, "I saw a grapevine in front of me. The vine had three branches that began to bud and blossom, and soon it produced clusters of ripe grapes. I was holding Pharaoh's wine cup in my hand, so I took a cluster of grapes and squeezed the juice into the cup. Then I placed the cup in Pharaoh's hand." "This is what the dream means," Joseph said. "The three branches represent three days. Within three days Pharaoh will lift you up and restore you to your position as his chief Cup-bearer.

Genesis 40:5-13

When the baker heard Joseph's interpretation of the cup-bearer's dream, he said to Joseph, "I had a dream, too. In my dream there were three baskets of white pastries stacked on my head. The top basket contained all kinds of pastries for Pharaoh, but the birds came and ate them from the basket on my head." "This is what the dream means," Joseph told him. "The three baskets also represent three days. Three days from now Pharaoh will lift you up and impale your body on a pole. Then birds will come and peck away at your flesh."

Genesis 40:16-19

Good news for one; tragic news for the other.

One would be restored to his position; the other was to die.

Along with this interpretation, Joseph makes one request to the cup-bearer: "When you are restored to your position, remember me. I didn't do anything to deserve to be here. I have been wrongly accused."

You can almost hear the desperation in his request. Joseph just wanted to be mentioned. *Remember me. Will you just allow my situation to be a passing thought? Will you just mention me to Pharaoh?* He was not demanding rights, not harboring bitterness, just simply and humbly asking to be remembered.

The third day was the Pharaoh's birthday, and just as Joseph said, the cup-bearer was restored and the baker was hanged.

But the cupbearer did not remember Joseph. He forgot him.

What a sad commentary. Joseph was forgotten. Again.

Have you ever felt that way? Like friends, family members, and colleagues have all forgotten you? Have you ever been forgotten by those you valued and in whom you have invested?

Have you wanted to throw in the towel? Quit believing,

quit hoping, and quit praying? Have you begun to think even God has forgotten you? Have you felt stuck in your own prison? If so, this is the moment you need to press in even more, pray more fervently, and believe more passionately.

This is the moment just before your breakthrough.

Although the prison was not a desirable place, Joseph kept faith alive. And right around the corner was his breakthrough. In God's economy, three steps forward and twenty steps back is progress! The truth is, you are not forgotten. God is very much aware of everything you are facing, everything you are struggling with, and every injustice you have been dealt. Not only has He not forgotten you, but He is with you.

The question is, is that enough?

CHAPTER NINETEEN

DESPERATELY WAITING

On a recent flight, I had boarded the plane according to my zone and was sitting in my seat waiting for takeoff. I was doing a last-minute check for email when we received the friendly reminder from the flight attendant to "turn your cell phone off." So I turned off my phone, placed it in my pocket, and got out a book to read, hoping to do something productive during my flight. As we pulled out of the gate, we received word over the intercom that we were in line for takeoff, but there would be a slight delay, as we were not number one in line.

As you might imagine, I was frustrated.

We've all been there. When it's time for us to fly, and we have checked off all the boxes brought to us courtesy of the TSA, we just want to get where we're going. To top it off, the little air conditioner wasn't working, and it was a stuffy, full flight. I sat there, sweating and feeling more frustrated until it hit me: What would typically take me about nine hours to drive is going to take me only two hours to fly, and I am irritated because it's a little warm and we're going to be delayed for 15 minutes.

Isn't this how we are?

On our daily commute to work we yell expletives about the traffic, as though it's a surprise. We avoid going to the doctor for fear of waiting forever in the waiting room. When informed by the hostess, "It'll be about a 15-minute wait," we look at the rest of our party and say, "I don't know, do y'all want to go to a different restaurant?"

We live in a culture that doesn't like to wait for anything. We don't get a gold star for patience. We want things done yesterday. We want the answer to the problem now. We want to heat it up in the microwave, pick it up at the drive through, and look it up on the Internet. We like progress and action, and waiting seems passive.

When it comes to the dreams God places inside our hearts, the last thing we want to do is wait. But how many of us are literally still paying for and cleaning up the messes we made by choosing to rush forward?

Throughout Scripture, we are presented with the concept of waiting on the Lord. We see in many passages that it is anything but a passive posture. I believe it is essential to the Christian life and to our growth as Christ followers to learn what it means to wait upon the Lord.

It's also essential to learn this as you pursue your dreams, because God wants to shape your heart. This concept is counter-intuitive to those of us who don't like to wait. But waiting is essential so God can do exceedingly and abundantly more through our lives than we could ever dream or imagine.

In the book of Samuel we find the story of a woman named Hannah who had to wait on the Lord. Hannah's husband, Elkanah, had another wife, named Peninnah.

Every year Elkanah traveled to a town called Shiloh to make a sacrifice at the temple. Each time Elkanah sacrificed an animal to the Lord, he gave portions of the meat to his wife Peninnah and to all her sons and daughters. This is important, because Peninnah had many sons and daughters, and women in that day found their value in having children, especially sons. But Elkanah gave a double portion of meat to Hannah, because he loved her even though she had not been able to give him any children of her own. So there was a very sweet love story going on there. But there was also rivalry.

Because Penninah was jealous of Elkanah's love, she mocked Hannah for not being able to have children. This went on year after year—the whole family traveling to Shiloh, Elkanah offering a sacrifice to God, giving a portion of meat to Penninah and her children, and giving a double portion to Hannah. And year after year, right there at the temple, Penninah would provoke and irritate Hannah until Hannah wept and wouldn't eat. This didn't happen just one time. This went on and on and on for Hannah.

It's bad enough that Hannah couldn't have children. This is a heartbreaking thing for any woman, and even worse in a culture where it determined her value as a woman. She had wept and prayed for God to change this for a long time. But Penninah's insults just made it worse.

Have you ever had someone mock you and nit-pick you and find your weak spot and exploit you like that? This happened to Hannah year after year. Imagine if you had to deal with the same hateful person at a big family holiday each year. This is how it was for Hannah.

Finally, the day came when it was more than she could bear. The Bible says,

> *Once, when they had finished eating and drinking in Shiloh, Hannah stood up. Now Eli, the priest, was sitting on a chair by the doorpost of the Lord's temple. In bitterness of soul, Hannah wept much and prayed to the Lord*
>
> 1 Samuel 1: 9-10

Have you ever been there?

Have you ever found yourself in the middle of a situation in which all you can do is weep and pray to the Lord? If so, you can relate to Hannah.

While weeping and praying near the door of the Temple, Hannah "made a vow, saying, 'Oh Lord Almighty, if You will only look upon Your servant's misery and remember me and not forget Your servant, but give her a son, then I will give him to the Lord for all the days of his life, and no razor will ever be used on his head.'"

Hannah was making a Nazarite vow on behalf of her not-yet-conceived child -- the same vow we read about in the story of Samson. The vow of the Nazarites is a pledge to live a devout life, abstain from wine or alcohol, never cut one's hair, and refrain from becoming unclean by touching a grave or a dead body. The man or woman who takes this vow and lives as a Nazarite is "set apart" -- different from others. The word "Nazarite" itself comes from the Hebrew root "nazir" which means "consecrated." So essentially, Hannah was saying, "God, if you will give me a son, I will set him apart to be yours."

Remember that Hannah had just finished her dinner and was near the door of the Temple where the high priest, Eli, was watching her.

"Eli observed her mouth," which moved in silent prayer as she wept and poured out her heart to God. Eli didn't know she was praying. He thought she was drunk, and rebuked her,

> *"How long will you keep getting drunk? Get rid of your wine."*

> *"Not so, my lord," Hannah replied. "I am a woman*

who is deeply troubled. I've not been drinking wine
or beer. I was pouring out my soul to the Lord. Do
not take your servant for a wicked woman. I've
been praying here out of my anguish and grief."

Samuel 1:14-16

Then Eli blessed her and said, "Go in peace, and may
the God of Israel grant you what you have asked of him"
(verse 17).

Now think about this with me: I don't think this is the
first time Hannah had prayed this prayer, do you? I don't
think it's the first time those words came out of her mouth.
She had been praying this prayer for years. She had been
waiting for God to answer.

Some of us don't like to wait five minutes for God, but
year after year, Hannah waited and prayed. After she
poured out her heart to Eli, he blessed her and said, "Go in
peace and may the God of Israel grant you what you have
asked of Him."

If you go on to read the rest of the story, you'll find out
that Hannah finally got the answer to her prayers. She had
her baby and named him Samuel, and he went on to write
the book of 1 Samuel which records this story.

Hannah brought Samuel back to Eli, as she had prom-
ised, and presented him to the Lord. Samuel grew up and
became a priest himself. He would eventually become the
very same Samuel who had the great honor of anointing

David the King of Israel. Samuel was used greatly in God's kingdom and in the history of the world, and you can read his life story in several books of the Bible. Hannah's prayers were answered and her dream came to fruition, to a greater degree than she could have asked or imagined.

But before she could hold that dream in her arms, Hannah had to wait for the Lord.

CHAPTER TWENTY

ACTIVELY WAITING

Has there been a moment in your life when you really needed God to intervene? When you really needed God to show up?

When you really needed to make progress?

When you really needed to hear the voice of God?

Or a solution from God?

Or an answer from God?

If you have not been there, you will be. We are all either in that place of desperation right now, waiting and begging God to intervene, or we have just come out of one of those seasons and we're brushing ourselves off and getting back on our feet, or we are about to go into such a season and we don't even know it yet. We are always in one of those three places. Life is a series of being in the storm, coming out of the storm, and going into the storm. It's just the cycle of life.

Like Hannah, we pray and pray for God to intervene. And

often God gently whispers, "Just wait."

We pray prayers like this:

"God, I need You to intervene and I need You to intervene right now. And furthermore, here's exactly how You should do it. I've got a great plan, and if you'll just follow it, everything will work out well. I've already thought through everything. I've got a good strategy for the big picture."

As if God can't see the bigger picture.

But that's the way we pray sometimes.

And often God says gently, "Hey, just wait. Wait for Me."

This feels like God is asking us to do nothing when it would make more sense to do something, anything, to change the situation. We want to take things into our own hands. We begin to make things happen.

We are smart.

We are capable.

We begin to kick down doors that God isn't ready to open for us, trying to find our own solutions.

And we face the consequences.

The truth is, waiting isn't passive at all. Waiting means to *hope* for, to *expect*, or to *trust*. In other words, when I become willing to wait on God rather than run ahead of Him, I'm saying, "God, I trust You."

The opposite is also true, isn't it? When we get ahead of God, we're saying, "God, I don't know if I can trust You to come through, so I'll just take care of it myself."

We never verbalize it that way because it doesn't sound

good. "God bless my food and my family, but I don't trust You, so I'll probably just take care of it myself" just doesn't seem holy.

Choosing to wait for God when we're desperate to find the answers now is taking an active stance to show our faith in God's plan.

Trust is a verb.

Trust is an action that I take.

It's saying, "God, I trust that at the end of the day, not only is Your plan better than mine, but Your plan has my best interest at heart."

God was thinking about you when He devised this plan. He was thinking about what would be best for you and considering what would prosper you, help you, encourage you, and allow you to go farther and faster than you ever dreamed in His kingdom.

Waiting for God says you believe all of that.

Waiting for God says you trust His timing.

God transcends time. He doesn't sync His calendar with His smart phone to make sure He's on time for all of His appointments. He sees the beginning to the end, all at the same time. We are only able to see time on a linear scale. We can only see things from here. God can see into billions of years from now. Because God is outside of time, He sees your birth at the same time He sees your death, and every moment that happens in between. He simultaneously sees the choices you make and the consequences of those choices.

Oddly enough, we think we have the big picture sometimes. But God is always on time, and waiting for Him requires learning to be content with His timing.

Being content means to be mentally and emotionally at peace. How many of us can say that we live there? I'd say very few of us.

Have you ever been on a lake early in the morning, before any boats have stirred it up? It looks just like glass. If I am at peace, my mind and emotions are as still as that lake. There may be a lot of chaos going on around me, but I am at peace.

To be content means I am also mentally and emotionally full. We want to see solutions to our problems, assuming the solutions will somehow fulfill us. We will get ahead of God in all kinds of situations because we think, If she'll just go out with me, then I'll feel fulfilled.

. . . *If we could just have this baby, our family would be complete.*

. . . *If I could just get that job, I would be financially stable.*

. . . *If I could just get accepted into that school, I'd be on the right track.*

God teaches us that we can be at peace, and fulfilled emotionally and mentally, even in a season of waiting—because of Him. The solution we so desperately want is not what will fulfill us. He alone will fulfill us.

This is why Paul wrote in his letter to the Philippians, "I have had everything and I have had nothing, but in all things I've learned to be content."

This is what separates the Christian from everyone else in the world: when we're emotionally and mentally full, our investments can blow up and we can still be at peace because our money isn't what fulfills us. That is when people look at you and say things like, "I don't know what you've got, and I don't know how you can walk through storms like this and stay content, but I want whatever it is."

You can reply, "It's because I trust God, and because I trust God, I have learned to be content in all things, whether I have a lot or a little."

When you get to the place in life where you say, "God, I'm content in You, no matter what happens," I believe God will open the door to your dream. You won't even need the dream to fulfill you. You will live that dream solely to be a blessing to other people. You will live that dream to show love to other people. You will live that dream to be generous to other people. You will begin to live from a philosophy of, "God, I want to love people more and need them less."

We need each other in the body of Christ, but I don't need you to fulfill me. I don't need my wife to fulfill me. I don't need a certain house or a certain car or a certain status or a certain outfit to fulfill me, because God fulfills me.

Do you know where that line of thinking positions me? I don't come to you needing to emotionally drain you in order to be emotionally full. I can love you out of the overflow of God Himself, in me. Isn't that beautiful?

When we learn to wait on the Lord, we learn to trust Him. When we trust Him, we learn to be content in His timing. When we are content in His timing, we live from a place of overflow of the love of God into the lives of others. I don't love because I need others to fulfill me. I only need Jesus to fulfill me and then from that fulfillment, I can pour His love into the lives of others.

CHAPTER TWENTY-ONE
LET IT COME TO YOU

We have been learning to wait for the Lord. We have learned that this is not a passive, sitting down, crossing your arms and tapping your foot posture. It is an active trust in God and an education in being content. So what do you do while you're waiting and learning?

I can think of three things:

First, we remain active. I know that sounds counter-intuitive. But we remain active to walk through only the doors God opens.

It might not be the solution you thought it would be.

It may not be the door you wanted to open.

But that part is not up to you.

Remember, God is outside of time. He knows much more than you and I know. We remain active to follow after God.

Second, we remain alert to what God is doing around us. How do we remain alert to God and to His voice? I don't know if He will audibly speak to you, but I do know He will speak to you through His Word.

Maybe you're in a season of waiting and you don't know what God wants you to do. I would ask you:

How much time have you spent reading the Bible?

How much time you have spent in prayer?

Prayer and praying through scripture allows you to remain alert to what God is doing.

Finally, we remain expectant. When you invite a guest over for dinner, you get everything cleaned up. You cook the meal. You light the candles. Then every few minutes, if you're like me, you go to the windows and glance out, or the kids will run to the door and ask, "Are they here yet?"

Why do we do that?

It's because we're expecting someone to show up.

This is exactly what God wants from us when we find ourselves in a season of waiting. He wants us to live with a heart of expectation. I believe that the atmosphere of expectancy creates fertile ground for miracles in our lives. I think God wants us to always be looking out the windows and standing by the door saying, "He's not here yet, but He's on His way."

I know He must be on His way, because I'm confident in God. I trust in God and I'm content and fulfilled, but I'm also expecting something. I'm expecting my breakthrough to be right around the corner. I'm expecting that the solution to my situation is coming soon. I'm expecting that as soon as I prayed my prayer, the answer was dispatched from Heaven, and is on its way.

I'm expecting Him.

Just as I would expect my invited guest to show up at my house, I'm going to expect the God of the Universe to whom I've cried out perhaps year after year, to come to my rescue. I'm going to expect there will come a moment, in His timing, when He will come through and provide the best solution. I'm simply going to expect it.

I think you might find your season of waiting could become the most productive season of your entire life if you learn to wait well.

But here's what I know: it's not easy.

You may be right in the middle of a season of waiting as you read this. Maybe like Hannah, you're waiting for a child, and you've prayed and prayed. And you're waiting.

Maybe you're waiting on a job, and you've prayed and cried out to God. Maybe you've even tried to get ahead of God and find a solution for yourself, but it blew up in your face—so you're waiting.

Maybe you have a prodigal child—a child who used to know and love God but who seems to have just walked away from it, and you've begged and you've prayed and you've waited for him to come home.

Maybe you're waiting for some direction. You're at a crossroads in your life and you're asking God, "Do I go right, or left, or straight? What do I do here?" You're waiting and you're praying.

Whatever you're waiting for, I believe God is speaking to you right now, saying gently, "Wait. Just wait." You have a choice to make. You can try to find a workaround on your own and walk away from the will of God in your life, but there will most certainly be consequences. It's up to you. God will never force Himself—or His plan—on you.

Or you can open your arms and say, "God, this may be the hardest thing I've ever done in my life, but I'm going to wait. I may take it back tonight. I may have to wake up tomorrow and say this all over again. But today, I'm going to try to wait for You. I'm expecting You to show up in this situation, in Your timing." You may have to do this over and over, until you really start actively waiting on the Lord.

I believe God wants you to know He's got something bigger going on in your life than you can see from where you are sitting. He's got your best interest at heart. If you'll just wait for Him—if you'll just learn to be content and find your fulfillment in Him rather than in everything around you—He will give you a solution that will be exceedingly, abundantly more than you could ever dream or imagine.

Maybe you're in that season of waiting right now, and you've been there for a long time. You thought surely by now God would have given you an answer. In your heart of hearts, you really don't want to get ahead of God, and you want to be content in Him, but you're in that season right now, and it's hard.

Today, you need to quit pushing against what God wants to do in you, let go and say, "God, I want to wait for You, but I need Your strength to live it out."

God knows your situation. He knows your story by heart. He knows every detail, emotion, and broken moment. He's seen every tear that has hit the ground. He's heard your every prayer. He will give you the strength, through His Spirit, to be able to wait for Him and trust that His timing is perfect.

Wait for God. Find contentment and fulfillment in Him alone.

Trust Him.

And expect Him to come through.

SECTION THREE
LIVING THE DREAM

CHAPTER TWENTY-TWO
OVERNIGHT SUCCESS

Have you ever been unable to sleep, so you turn on the TV and find every channel showing a get-rich-quick scheme or a miracle weight loss remedy? These are rampant in late night television, magazine advertisements, and social media, because marketers know our culture is obsessed with quick turn-arounds, immediate results, and putting forth very little work to gain a high return.

We want it fast, we want it now, and we want to do the minimum amount of work to get it. This is why fast food chains and frozen food manufacturers are so successful. It's why the number of homes with microwave ovens has grown from 12% of households in 1971 to over 90% of households today. We want to buy it now and pay for it later. We don't want to wait for it, work for it, or worry about it.

But when it comes to character—having our hearts shaped by God—there is no such thing as an overnight success. Character doesn't come easily and it doesn't come quickly. It is formed in a slow cooker rather than a microwave. This is true for us, and it was true for Joseph.

Much time had passed in Joseph's life during which he could have become bitter, disgruntled, or defeated.

He had been sold into slavery.

He had been falsely accused.

He had been imprisoned.

He had been forgotten.

And all the while, Joseph had done nothing wrong. But instead of growing angry, Joseph allowed God to grow his character. And now we find Joseph in a moment of testing.

God wasn't testing Joseph's skill. Obviously Joseph had skill; he had found favor and risen to power everywhere he had gone. God had already tested Joseph's faith in his God-designed purpose and his ability to remain faithful while doing a job that was beneath his capacity and worth. And now God was testing Joseph's faithfulness.

Two full years had passed for Joseph in prision, with no word from anyone.

For two full years, Joseph hoped the cupbearer would remember him.

It had been two years of the same environment.

Two years of the same routine.

Time has the ability to strengthen our resolve, give us perspective, and allow us to mature. But time can also talk us out of what we know God is calling us to do. Time can be a killer. As the Righteous Brothers sang, *Time goes by so slowly . . . and time can do so much . . .*

Time can cause us to second-guess what God is saying.

Time can rob our passion for what God has birthed in our hearts.

Time can create an opportunity for delayed obedience, which is really disobedience.

What has time talked you out of doing?

It's time to take action. It's time to re-engage in what the voice of God has already made evident to you. It's time to stop killing time.

Joseph had been waiting for two full years. What a long time for Joseph to have his hope deferred! Proverbs 13:12 says, "Hope deferred makes the heart sick, but a longing fulfilled is a tree of life." It is perseverance in a season of waiting that prepares us to prosper when God's dream for us is fulfilled.

Joseph did not grow bitter or resentful. In spite of all he had been through, he did not throw in the towel on God's dream for him. This was an opportunity for Joseph to prove his character—a character that had been shaped through abandonment and betrayal and slavery and false accusations and prison. A character that had been shaped by God.

And now, increase was imminent in the life of Joseph.

The moment of Joseph's promotion marked the finished shaping of the heart of the dreamer. The lessons set aside for Joseph had been completed, and they came to fruition at the exact moment the plans of God's providence were matured.

CHAPTER TWENTY-THREE

WHAT A DIFFERENCE A DAY MAKES

Two years after Joseph had been forgotten by the cup-bearer, the Pharaoh dreamed he was standing by the Nile River when out of the water, seven sleek, fat, healthy cows emerged. The healthy cows grazed among the weeds on the bank of the Nile until another seven cows appeared. The seven new cows were clearly malnourished; they were ugly and bony. The seven thin cows ate the seven fat ones, but remained skinny and scrawny, as though they had eaten nothing.

The Pharaoh awoke disturbed, and went back to sleep. This time, he had another dream, in which seven healthy heads of grain grew on a single stalk. After them, another seven heads of grain, dried up and windblown, sprouted up. The seven thin heads of grain swallowed up the seven healthy heads of grain. Again, the Pharaoh woke up and was deeply troubled.

As was customary, the Pharaoh called on the wise men and magicians of Egypt to give meaning to his dream, but they were unable to do so. If anyone should have been able to interpret Pharaoh's dream, it would have been these men. It was their job to advise and reveal mysteries, but they had no answers. Their inability to interpret these dreams was not a negative reflection of their own abilities, but a spotlight on the providence of God at work in the life of Joseph.

If God has destined you to do something, it is for you and you alone to do. No matter who is in front of you, no matter who has more expertise, more connections, or more privilege, God will clear the path, open the doors, and make a way for you to fulfill His unique purpose for you.

When the magicians and wise men came up empty, God caused the cup-bearer to remember the Hebrew slave he had met in jail two years before.

And he spoke up.

Finally.

Two long years after his promise to remember Joseph, the cup-bearer remembered. He shared with Pharaoh how Joseph had interpreted his dream when he was imprisoned —as well as the dream of the chief baker—and how both interpretations happened exactly as Joseph had predicted.

This one recollection of the cup-bearer was all it took. Pharaoh sent for Joseph to be brought to him. After Joseph was cleaned up, he was presented to the Pharaoh.

This was the moment in which Joseph's preparation was

about to intersect with his destiny.

God had planned, exceedingly, abundantly and above all that Joseph could have dreamed or imagined. And all this time, God had been shaping Joseph's heart and character, preparing him to be able to receive this exceeding abundance. Joseph had gone through what Zechariah 13:9 calls the refining fire of God so that he would be prepared for this moment.

Joseph couldn't have prepared for this on his own.

Joseph couldn't have planned for this in his wildest dreams.

But God, in His mercy, was with Joseph.

Years of preparation had gone into this moment.

Years of God shaping Joseph, the dreamer.

Years of God growing Joseph's integrity, humility, and confidence in God.

Years of God peeling away Joseph's pride and bringing him to a place in which he would live with one purpose and one motive only—for God's glory.

Years of God building into Joseph a character that says, "in every situation, in every circumstance, I will reflect the nature and the character of my God."

There is no such thing as an overnight success. There is no overnight rise to power. Behind any God-given success, there are years of shaping and molding and preparation. I am a firm believer that if a person seems to be an overnight success, they will not be able to stand when their moment comes and they will become an instant failure.

Let's face it: you can't get ahead of God's process. There is no way you can beat Him. So you might as well embrace it. God's timing is perfect. God's plan is precise. God's purpose is His glory through you and for your good.

After all this time, Joseph had learned who the Author of his providence really was. Joseph was not about to take credit for God's work. He stood before Pharaoh with a godly confidence -- a confidence in the One who had brought him to this place and who had instilled the character he needed to succeed in this moment.

The Pharaoh said to Joseph, "I hear you can interpret dreams."

And Joseph's response was amazing: "I cannot do it."

Those four words summed up Joseph's entire journey prior to this point. Joseph had come to a place in which he realized his life, his abilities, and his destiny were all wrapped up in God's power.

Joseph got it!

Joseph was ready for God to unveil a dream so great he didn't even have the capacity to dream it himself. God had dreamed it on his behalf.

And Joseph was ready to receive it.

These words—"I cannot do it"—didn't come from a head knowledge based on the stories and experiences of others. These words didn't come from a desire to give a nice little Jesus-juke "God-answer."

These words were uttered from lips that had cracked due to lack of water in a pit.

These words were formed from a heart that had experienced loneliness, injustice, and betrayal.

These words were spoken with conviction and passion by a man who was convinced they were true.

Everything Joseph had believed this whole time was at this very moment becoming real.

This is where God wants to bring us—a place of total and complete dependence on Him. The moment we arrive in that place is the moment God opens the door and the moment we know it is God who is bringing us through. It is God who deserves the credit and glory, and it is God alone who will see us through.

When we get to an "I cannot do it" place, we are perfectly positioned to see the glory of our great God revealed in our lives in ways we have never dreamed possible.

Joseph said, "I cannot do it. . . but God will." Those three words change the dynamic of any situation.

I don't have enough money, but God will. . .

I don't have the courage, but God will. . .

I don't have support, but God will. . .

My kids don't love Jesus, but God will . . .

I'm not good enough, but God will. . .

Everyone thinks I am crazy, but God will. . .

I don't know how I'm going to get through this situation, but God will. . .

God changes the dynamic of every situation, the landscape of every battle, and the perspective of every obstacle. Not only is God able and powerful, He is also willing to move on your behalf.

Joseph could speak with such confidence because he must have known God is drawn to a contrite spirit—to a life that embraces complete dependence on Him. Joseph said, "God will give Pharaoh the answer he desires."

And God does just that.

Joseph explains to the Pharaoh, "The seven healthy cows represent seven years of prosperity in the land, but the seven unhealthy cows represent seven years of famine that will come after that."

Because Joseph had nothing to prove and no one to impress, he gave Pharaoh an honest, yet not completely positive answer. He added a plan with which to prepare--a plan no doubt given to Joseph by God Himself in the moment Joseph really needed it.

Pharaoh responded, "Where else can I find a man in whom is the Spirit of God?" Pharaoh recognized the hand of God on Joseph's life and gave the job to Joseph. No one except the Pharaoh would be greater than Joseph in the land. At the age of thirty, Joseph was put in charge of the whole land of Egypt. Pharaoh dressed him in royal clothes, gave him a ring, and gave him a wife. You may have read this story hundreds of times or may be reading it for the first time today, but don't miss the significance and symbolism of these things God lavished on Joseph. God redeemed all that Joseph had lost:

The royal clothes replaced Joseph's lost coat.

The wife returned a family to Joseph.

The royal ring restored Joseph's authority.

Joseph had gone from the prison to the palace—and he was prepared.

Anything is possible in your life when you don't care who gets the glory! When Joseph was given his moment to shine, he gave God all the glory. As a result, Joseph found prosperity in the land of his suffering.

But that's not all.

The Pharaoh executed Joseph's plan to save food and grain aggressively during the seven years of abundance. When famine struck for the next seven years, just as Joseph had predicted, Egypt was ready. The famine was severe and reached countries beyond Egypt. The other countries had not prepared for the famine as Egypt had, and soon all the world came to Egypt to buy grain from Joseph.

During this time Joseph's father Jacob learned there was grain in Egypt, and sent his sons—Joseph's brothers—to buy food for their survival. He sent all of his sons except the youngest, Benjamin, who was Joseph's full brother. Jacob had believed all these years that Joseph was dead, and for all Joseph's brothers knew, he was still a slave somewhere.

When Joseph's brothers arrived in Egypt, they were brought before Joseph to purchase their grain. They did not recognize him and bowed down to him with their faces to the ground.

But Joseph recognized them.

Can you imagine how Joseph felt in that moment? His dream was coming true right before his eyes. He had no idea how it would take place when he first had that dream so long ago. He pretended not to know them and sent them home to bring back their youngest brother—*his* brother—Benjamin.

Through a long string of events, Joseph's brothers returned with Benjamin, and eventually Joseph revealed his identity to them all. As he did so, he forgave them for what they had done to him.

Joseph knew that his family bowing before him was a small blip on the radar compared to what God had planned. God used Joseph during the famine to save not only Egypt, but the whole known world.

His dream had come to fruition, his family was reunited, and Joseph's life made an impact on history for generations to come.

CHAPTER TWENTY-FOUR
GOD'S DREAM FOR YOU

Throughout this book, we have discussed positioning our-selves in a place to begin living our dreams. Have you ever paused to consider God's dream? Humor me for a moment: if we were to ask God to tell us the great dream in His heart, what would it be?

What is that thing that drives the passion of God?

What is that thing around which God has orchestrated and ordered all of creation and all of eternity?

What was the reason for Jesus' time on this earth?

I believe its sentiment is found in the words Joseph spoke to his brothers while revealing his identity to them. In Genesis Chapter 45, we find Joseph's brothers, recently returned to Egypt and bowing before Joseph. They know he is a ruler in Egypt, second only to the Pharaoh, but they are unaware of who he really is. Joseph says to them, "Come close to me. I am your brother Joseph, the one you sold into

Egypt! And now, do not be distressed and do not be angry with yourselves for selling me here, because it was to save lives that God sent me ahead of you."

In this statement, Joseph is acknowledging that it was the will of God and the purpose of God that brought him to this moment. And the purpose of God—the dream God had for Joseph—was to save lives.

Isn't this the dream of God for all of us?

Isn't this why Jesus came?

I would propose that the dream of God is not just for your church or your community or your town or even this country. It's for the entire world. I can also tell you it's an eternal dream. It is for everyone who has ever lived and everyone who ever will live, regardless of gender, race, color, background, or socioeconomic status. God's dream is for everyone.

God's dream is a dream for you. I would go so far as to say that if your own dream does not advance God's dream, then it's not a God-given dream. The dream of God should be so imprinted on our hearts that everything we do begins to flow in the direction of His dream.

We find God's dream in the words of Jesus. His dream, as quoted in Luke 19:10, is to seek and to save that which was lost. The dream that is in the heart of God, the rhyme and the reason behind everything Jesus did while on earth, was to seek and to save those who were far from Him. In other words, the dream of God is about people.

People who have blown it.

People who have messed up.

People who have made poor choices.

People who have made a mess of their lives.

People who think they have it all together.

People who know they don't have it all together.

People who have lived anything but a holy life.

People like me.

People like you.

God's dream is about people who are far from God. His dream is to find them and to save them.

It's to seek them out. It's to pursue them. God is on this mission of pursuing people. Have you ever thought about that?

I live near our nation's capital, and one of the more popular sights there is the Lincoln Memorial. You may have seen this in movies or photos, but when you actually stand in front of the Lincoln Memorial, you feel about the size of an ant. When some people think of God, I think they picture Him made out of marble, sitting coldly on a chair about the size of Abe's.

But God is not up on some high and lofty throne looking down at us as though we were ants. The God of the universe has a dream in His heart, and His mission is to pursue people who have blown it. That's all of us. God is pursuing humanity. He is seeking us out. He wants to rescue us, to erase our sins, to give us brand-new beginnings and brand-new starts. He wants to make our lives new.

This is what God is about.

If you and I have really been given a God-ordained dream, then somewhere in our dream, we will want the same thing He wants. Something in our dream will be about seeking and saving the lost. It will be about getting in on the mission of Jesus because when that happens—when God finds us and we connect with Him, enter into a relationship with Him, and accept His forgiveness—we return to the Garden.

You've heard of Adam and Eve. Even if you've never read a page in the Bible, you've probably seen the intro to *Desperate Housewives*. You have some idea of what happened in the story, but here it is for you in a nutshell: in the book of Genesis, Adam and Eve lived in the Garden of Eden. God had already created everything, including Adam and Eve.

When God created Adam and Eve, He said, "We're going to create them in our image." Adam and Eve and all humans after them are the image-bearers of God. We've all been created in God's likeness, and there is a seed of greatness inside each one of us.

Adam and Eve had a perfect relationship with God. They walked with Him in the cool of the day. Genesis indicates they communicated face-to-face with him. I don't know what they talked about, but they had audible, verbal conversations with one another. How amazing is that?

There were no broken dreams, or heartaches, or pain in

the garden. There were no natural disasters in the Garden. There was no terrorism in the garden. There was only peace. There was only a perfection we can't possibly understand or even imagine. Genesis 2 says Adam and Eve were naked but were not ashamed. There was no sense of shame in them at all. They walked around like this with one another, and they walked around like this with God, and felt perfectly comfortable.

What a setup, right? Adam and Eve lived in paradise. All of their needs were met. They had plenty to eat. They didn't worry about what to wear or what they looked like. They did not have to commute, or even work at all. They had no bills, no mortgage, and no deadlines. They hung out, in person, with God Himself. They had nothing to worry about. At all.

Then it happened. In Genesis, we read paradise was lost:

> *Now the serpent was more crafty than any of the wild animals the LORD God had made. He said to the woman, "Did God really say, 'You must not eat from any tree in the garden'?" The woman said to the serpent, "We may eat fruit from the trees in the garden, but God did say, 'You must not eat fruit from the tree that is in the middle of the garden, and you must not touch it, or you will die.'"*
>
> Genesis 3:1-3

The snake embodied Satan, the enemy of our souls. In

this scene, Satan simply did what he always does when he's trying to tempt us: he twists the words of God in order to make us question the intentions of God.

> *'You will not surely die,' the serpent said to the woman, 'for God knows that when you eat of it, your eyes will be opened and you will be like God, knowing good and evil.'*
>
> Genesis 3:5

Satan's scheme has not changed. He tries to convince us, when God says no to something, that God is really hiding something better from us. He still uses the same tactics to entice us to disobey God.

When I was a kid, I hated going to bed. I just knew a house party broke out whenever I went to bed and I was going to miss something fun or important. I would bet my Mom and Dad were breaking out pizza and soda and candy galore as soon as my eyes were closed. I imagined Skittles covering the living room floor five inches deep, and my parents were sending me to bed because they didn't want me to get in on the good stuff.

When Satan tempts us, that's exactly what he tries to make us think. He tries to persuade us into believing, *God really doesn't want what's best for you. He doesn't want you to get in on the good stuff.* The enemy knows what we believe drives our behavior, so he targets our beliefs. This is why he told Eve, "God knows if you eat that fruit, you're going to have something God doesn't want you to have."

So Eve began to believe this lie. She didn't want to miss out on anything, so she fell for the trap and ate the only thing in the whole garden that was forbidden.

> *When the woman saw that the fruit of the tree was good for food and pleasing to the eye, and also desirable for gaining wisdom, she took some and ate it. She also gave some to her husband, who was with her, and he ate it. Then the eyes of both of them were opened, and they realized they were naked.*
>
> Genesis 3: 6-7

In the chapter prior to this, Adam and Eve were naked but not ashamed. Now, realizing they are naked, they try to sew fig leaves together to make coverings for themselves.

For the first time in the history of the world, humanity experiences shame.

> *Then the man and his wife heard the sound of the LORD God as he was walking in the garden in the cool of the day, and they hid from the LORD God among the trees of the garden. But the LORD God called to the man, "Where are you?" He answered, "I heard you in the garden, and I was afraid be-*

cause I was naked; so I hid"

Genesis 3 :8-10

Just one chapter ago, Adam was walking with God, talking with Him face-to-face. He had the honor of having an intimate knowledge of God. His experience was that of peace, no broken promises, no broken relationships, no shame.

Now he's afraid.

I was naked; so I hid.

In one moment, the story goes from paradise to paradise lost.

CHAPTER TWENTY-FIVE
PARADISE RESTORED

God created humans in order to have a relationship with us. I'm not talking about religion. I'm talking about relationship. Religion wants to give you rules and regulations and boxes to check off in order to please God. But God sent His Son here so that you could actually have a relationship. With Him.

So you could know Him personally.

So you could have His peace and His power in your life.

But God also created man and woman so He could express love to us. There has to be an object of your affection if you are to truly love. God created us to be the objects of His love.

He was not lonely or in need of a relationship; God is complete within Himself. He is not emotionally needy. He did not create humanity because He needed more friends on Facebook. God is perfect, and perfectly complete, all by

Himself.

God wanted to create people to whom He could express His love, because He is a loving God.

The ability to love and receive love from someone requires this thing called free will. You cannot demand love and then believe that what you are receiving is real. You can't threaten someone in order to gain his love. A threatened person may show you some kind of affection out of fear, but it will not be love. You cannot demand real love. Real love must be given.

True love is given freely.

If I give my wife flowers on our anniversary, and after she thanks me I tell her, "Well, it's written in the book of what husbands should do. 'Bring flowers on anniversary.' I have checked the box. We are now going out to dinner. That is box number two on the anniversary rules list. I will pay for it, which is box number three." Do you think that would feel like love to her? It wouldn't, because it isn't. It's just checking off boxes of what husbands are "supposed to do." Love that is forced or demanded is not true love.

In order for love to be real, it must be a choice made over an equally possible choice of rejection. When I give someone the choice to love me, I also give that person the choice to reject me. God gave us the ability to choose, which means He also gave us the ability to reject Him.

God created Adam and Eve in His own image and breathed life into them. He gave them a choice to love or reject Him. In Genesis chapter 3, God's own creation chose to turn their backs on him. In that moment, something entered into the equation that had never been there before. Something entered the world that changed everything.

The moment Adam and Eve disobeyed God, sin entered the world and the relationship between Creator and creation was severed. God is a loving God, but God is also a just God, because without justice He would not truly love. Love and justice are not opposed. They balance and give credit to each other. Because God is love, He has to be just. Because He is just, He is a God of great love and mercy.

Being just, God had to deal with the sin that had entered the world. God had created us to be in relationship with Him, but the relationship was broken by sin. There was suddenly an imbalance of justice caused by the offense, and there had to be a payment to reconcile the account and bring it back into balance.

There was a high price to pay. Verse 23 says, "So the Lord God banished (Adam) from the Garden of Eden, to work the ground from which he had been taken (Genisis 3:23)."

Adam and Eve were kicked out of the garden. Everything changed.

They had to work.

They experienced pain.

They felt the frustration of human relationships.

They were ashamed.

We may wish this story had a different ending, but it

couldn't have. God is holy. If He were anything other than holy, you wouldn't want to serve Him, and if He simply overlooked sin, He wouldn't be holy.

The relationship was broken and Adam and Eve were kicked out of the garden.

This so perfectly describes us, doesn't it? We, too, have a severed relationship with God. We, too, have experienced the effect of sin. If your heart has ever been broken, you have experienced the effect of sin. If you have ever experienced pain, you have experienced the effect of sin. If you have had to work hard to pay your bills or watched a loved one pass away, you have experienced the effect of sin.

Sin affected all of creation. There were no hurricanes or earthquakes or eroding of the shores before sin entered the world. In a very real sense, sin was a natural disaster. It changed everything.

We have not only experienced the effects of sin; we ourselves are sinful. We don't have to try at sin; we're just naturally good at it. That's why it's called a "sin nature." The bad news is, we were born with it. It's in us. Because of that, the relationship with our Holy God has been broken. So what do we do?

Some try religion.

If I try harder . . .

If I do better . . .

If I turn over a new leaf . . .

If I make more commitments . . .

If I attend church regularly . . .

If I drink less beer . . .

If I'm nicer to my wife . . .

If I stop cussing . . .

If I check all these boxes . . . maybe I will be able to mend the relationship with God and be in right standing with Him again.

But all religion does is leave us confused and frustrated.

The Apostle Paul wrote in the book of Romans that the penalty for sin is death. The only way to right the wrong is for someone to die. And even though the relationship is broken, God's love and the pursuit of us has never stopped.

God knew there was nothing we could do to right the wrongs affected by sin. There is no amount of good we can do that could possibly make us holy enough. I've heard people say they hope when they get to Heaven their good deeds outweigh their bad behavior. But there's no scale, and even if there were, our good would be weighed against God's perfection and we would lose, every time.

God knew there would be no way for us to do enough or be good enough to restore our broken relationship with Him. So He did the unthinkable. God had a dream to seek and to save the lost. The only way that could be done was for someone to pay the penalty. Because His dream was to have a relationship with you, He gave His only son, Jesus, to pay the death penalty on our behalf. Jesus became your substitute and my substitute, and made retribution for all of our sin.

All of it.

Jesus took the punishment with which we were sentenced. He went to the cross and allowed nails to be put into His hands and feet. He allowed a crown of thorns to be shoved onto His head and He shed His blood and died on the cross so that our sins would be forgiven. He came to seek and to save the lost. He came to pursue you.

So that we would be made clean in God's eyes.

So that we could have a right relationship with God.

Because that is God's dream.

You don't have to pay the penalty for your sin if you'll just trust in what He did for you on the cross. That is all that is needed to repair the break in the relationship and close the distance between you and God. Jesus has made a way for you to have a personal relationship with God, and that may be the very reason you are reading this right now. God's original design was to express this great love to you. Sin broke the relationship, but He is not giving you up that easily.

Jesus made a way to restore and reconcile the relationship.

Jesus made a way to wash away all of your sin, as if it never even took place.

Jesus made a way to remake you—to redeem you.

Jesus made a way for all of that on the cross.

The cross is the greatest symbol of God's dream because

it held the pathway to God. The cross is not just a nice trinket to wear around your neck. It's the greatest gift ever given to humanity. It is the symbol of the suffering Jesus willingly paid so that you could be reconciled to God.

Maybe as you're reading this, you feel more like you are a part of the lost crowd than the found crowd. You know in your heart if you're far from God. You know in your heart if your relationship with God is not where it needs to be. Perhaps you feel like you're more separated from God than reconciled to God. If that is how you're feeling, I've got some great news for you. Jesus said that anyone who calls on His name will be found.

Anyone.

It doesn't matter what you were doing last night or last week or last month or all of last year. Jesus said anyone who calls on His Name will be saved. Anyone!

Anyone who will believe.

Jesus' death wasn't the end of the story. God raised Him from the dead three days later. He lives to prove that we, too, will have eternal life in Heaven if we will accept His free gift. The book of Romans says that if you confess with your mouth that Jesus is Lord and believe in your heart that God raised Him from the dead, you will be saved.

What does that mean? It means you'll be found. It means you'll be washed clean of anything that stains you or soils the perfection in which you were meant to live. It means that all your sins will be removed—erased. It means that, in part, you can return to the garden and have that kind of communication and intimacy and relationship with God.

That is His dream.

The great gift of Jesus is being offered to you right now. If you want to accept it—if you want to move from the lost crowd to the found crowd—you can do that right now.

There is a simple prayer you can pray, wherever you are, right now. There's nothing magical in this prayer, but if you mean it and you believe it, I believe God will do what He said He would do, and He'll find you. He'll save you.

Prayer is simply having a conversation with God. He has been waiting to hear from you . . .

Dear Jesus, I confess that I'm lost. I know you have been running after me and today I want to stop running. I believe Your Son Jesus died on the cross for me and that He rose again, three days later, so that I could be found. Today, I turn from my sin and place my faith in Jesus. Lord, I give You my life. Thank You for seeking and saving me. In Jesus' Name. Amen.

Having prayed that prayer, you are found. You are saved. You are washed clean.

You are new.

This is your first step toward returning to the Garden and finding that connection with God. And this is your first step toward living the dream.

My prayer for all of us is that we would we be forever engaged in living God's dream of seeking and saving the lost.

BONUS MATERIAL

Any time I talk about my father's illness, people always ask how the story ends.

Dad battled this rare disease for seven years, and much of the time no one had an answer or even a diagnosis for him. We took him to every major medical institution you can think of and no one was able to help us, until one day when a new doctor moved to our little town in east Tennessee. Years of suffering through doctor after doctor left my Dad reluctant to try another one, but my mother, being in the medical profession, heard about this doctor and finally convinced my Dad to go see him.

That doctor's appointment became a divine appointment, as within minutes the doctor diagnosed my Dad and began a treatment regimen that would improve my Dad's health. However, in the seventh year of this disease things began to go downhill again, which culminated on the night that I shared about in the introduction of this book. Shortly after that night, my Dad was taken to a hospital in Louisiana where doctors who specialized in this disease gathered to determine a solution. It was there that they took him off all the medicines he had been taking. And it was there that God healed him.

Completely. Miraculously.

Healed him.

Dad tells the story about sitting before the top medical professionals in this field of study and being asked, "Reverend Floyd, do you believe in divine healing?"

Of course my Dad responded, "Yes I do, and I believe in the Divine Healer. His name is Jesus."

And Dad went on to talk about Jesus.

I just wonder if, like Joseph, all that Dad had gone through was preparing him for that moment. I wonder if, like Paul, Dad went through a terrible storm in order to arrive at an opportunity to give glory to the Divine Healer in front of people who might never have heard about Him.

I often stand on the stage of our church, where I have the privilege of preaching to thousands of people each week, and think the same thing about myself. In light of all that we experienced as a family during Dad's sickness, could it be that I was being prepared for this?

I think so!

ACKNOWLEDGEMENTS

It is only because of the grace of God that I am able to offer this work to you. This book isn't the result of an intellectual exercise, but rather the experience of my journey. Thank you Jesus for the privilege of being called Yours.

To the Lifepoint Church Family, thank you for being an incredibly passionate group of faith-filled people. Your passion for Jesus and for His mission is contagious. Together we truly are living the dream.

To my assistant Kristen Schlee, thank you for the late nights and early mornings you spent pouring over this manuscript, all the while keeping my world in order. You are truly a gift to my family and to our church.

To the Lifepoint staff, you are world class. There is no other group of people with whom I would want to live this dream! I love you and believe the best is yet to come.

To my wife Tammie and our children, Owen and Faith, Thank you for your unending support throughout the process of producing this book. Thank you for believing in me and speaking courage into me in the moments I needed it the most. I can't believe we get to do this together. I love you more than words.

CPSIA information can be obtained
at www.ICGtesting.com
Printed in the USA
BVHW080801080119
537116BV00002B/6/P